SHE'S SELLING
WHAT?!

SHE'S SELLING WHAT?!

A SKEPTICAL HUSBAND'S GUIDE TO SUPPORTING HIS NETWORK MARKETING WIFE

TIM FARRANT

Published by Forefront Books.

Cover Design by Bruce Gore, Gore Studio Inc.
Interior Design by Bill Kersey, KerseyGraphics
Author Photo by Erica Manning, ericamanningphoto.com

ISBN: 9781948677240 print
ISBN: 9781948677257 e-book
ISBN: 9781948677264 audio

DEDICATION

For Beckie, the most beautiful, fearless, inspiring woman I know.

The way you have navigated the curveballs life has thrown at you with grit and grace is amazing to watch.

Thank you for always supporting my dreams and believing in me more than I believe in myself.

I love that we get to do this life together!

ACKNOWLEDGEMENTS

WRITING THIS BOOK HAS BEEN QUITE A CRAZY JOURNEY, AND IT would have been impossible to complete it without the encouragement, guidance, and (at times) the kick in the butt I needed to see this through. While many people have supported me and cheered me on throughout the process, I'd like to say a special word of thanks to the following people who stood by me, worked with me, and made this dream a reality.

My wife, Beckie, without whose actual business success this book could never have been written. You are an amazing wife, mother, supporter of my dreams, and champion of the things God has called me to pursue. We've come a long way, babe, and we're just getting started!

My son, Isaac, whose encouraging words are infectious, and my daughter, Kayla, who spent hours listening to my stories and helping me think through marketing strategies. You both are world-changers, and I'm proud to be your dad!

My parents, who modeled a God-fearing, healthy marriage to me. You taught me to work hard, think strategically about everything, and be comfortable in who God made me to be. This book is only possible because of the values you instilled in me.

Allen Harris, my developmental editor, whose guidance helped me move from being a scared first-time author to a confident writer who trusts my own voice and content. I can't imagine trying to pull this off without you.

Jonathan Merkh, my publisher, who seems to know everyone in Nashville and beyond. You have been so patient with me, and the connections and advice you have given me have created the runway needed to make this book a success.

Keith Minier, my friend and pastor, who is responsible for more fortune-cookie phrases in this book than people will ever know. Every chapter has your fingerprints on it, and I'm grateful for the support you have been to me in this journey.

Laurie Roe, who told me I could do this even when I didn't believe I could. You held my hand through the first steps in this process and gave me the courage to do what felt impossible. This wouldn't have gotten off the ground without you.

And finally, Beckie's amazing team. You ladies (and your husbands) are rock stars! Thank you for letting me use your stories of success and failure in this book. Your openness and vulnerability are an inspiration to others. Let's keep changing our families' futures and strengthening our marriages by building crazy-successful businesses with this amazing product that is helping so many people!

I am extremely grateful for you all!

TABLE OF CONTENTS

INTRODUCTION

I STILL WASN'T SURE ABOUT ALL THIS.

It was February 2018, and I was on my way to a free, week-long beach vacation to Punta Cana with my wife, Beckie. She had been with a network-marketing company for a year and a half and had busted her tail trying to get it off the ground. Beckie doesn't do anything halfway; she *killed it* over those initial months. As a reward for her early success, she and I got a free, all-expenses-paid trip to a fantastic beach resort. Not bad, right?

As excited as I was about a trip to the beach with my wife (and no kids!), I was pretty nervous. There would be three hundred top-performing people on this trip—most of them women—and they'd have their husbands with them. I knew I'd be expected to hang out with them, go to workshops, and listen to a lot of presentations. While I was impressed at the income my wife had generated in this business, I still had a lot of questions about how it all worked, what future there was in it, and how the other husbands felt about it. I didn't realize at the time how much of an impact that getaway would have on my wife's businesses—not to mention our marriage.

The first dinner group session kicked off an entire week of hearing essentially the same story again and again. Woman after woman took the podium to share her story of building her business. She'd start by telling us how she entered the business herself, usually at the invitation of a friend or family member. Then, at some point in practically every story, the speaker would talk about her husband's reaction. It was rarely good. She'd describe how unsupportive, resistant, or outright belligerent he was about the whole thing. She would talk about the endless questions he asked in the beginning. Occasionally, we even heard about how some husbands openly mocked their wives' businesses.

Of course, the speaker's husband was always sitting in the audience during all this, so she'd shoot him a sharp look and grin—just enough to let the crowd know who he was. We'd look over at the guy, laughing with him as he gave us a sheepish, goofy look and shrugged his shoulders, admitting that he wasn't as supportive as he should have been. Every man in the room knew how he felt; we *all* approached our wives' businesses with a mix of serious doubt and skepticism early on.

But, as the speaker continued, she'd talk about the point when her husband got on board with the business. It was often months later, but eventually her success brought him around. It was hard to laugh off her business when her "silly network-marketing thing" doubled, tripled, or quadrupled his own full-time salary! A lot of these husbands had actually left their own jobs to focus on their wives' businesses—many of which were earning more than $500,000 per year.

After hearing more than a dozen of these same stories of reluctant husbands throughout the week, I began to see a huge opportunity. I told Beckie we could revolutionize her business if we started teaching the women on her team how to get their husbands involved early on. For Beckie and me, this wasn't just a business or financial issue; it was a marriage issue. We hated hearing about how so many marriages struggled during the early days of the wife's network-marketing business. We sympathized with her team members' stories of unsupportive or critical husbands. Having been there myself, I knew where these guys were coming from. They weren't bad husbands at all; they just didn't trust the business and weren't sure how to support their wives.

All that marital stress eventually took a toll on the women's businesses. Beckie and I had lost count of the women she had brought onto her team who had fallen away or given up simply because they couldn't handle the negativity and pressure their husbands were putting on them. In our experience, it seemed like the typical husband was fine with his wife building a network-marketing business—as long as it didn't cost them financially or interfere with *his* life at all. As soon as he was inconvenienced or asked to help, his attitude would change. Then, when he realized how much time, money, and energy his wife was putting into the business, he was ready for her to pull the plug. Sadly, many women gave in to the pressure, often feeling guilty or foolish about getting so involved in what her husband called a "waste of time and money."

Beckie and I realized that if we could get both spouses on the same page quickly, we could save their businesses *and* help their marriages through the building phase. So, sitting in our hotel room in Punta Cana toward the end of that week, I scoured Amazon for resources. It seemed like such an obvious need; I assumed I'd find a dozen books on the topic. Instead, I found nothing—not one single book for helping husbands understand and support their network-marketing wives. I went home shocked that no one had written anything on the topic and frustrated that we didn't have a resource to give Beckie's team members.

Over the next few months, as Beckie continued to build her business, I became obsessed with how husbands reacted to their wives' new businesses. I watched as dozens of women quit the team because of their husbands' intentional sabotage, relentless pressure, unwillingness to help, and snide remarks. Once I had identified the glaring problem, it was impossible not to see it everywhere. And, honestly, it was tough to watch over and over again, knowing I once had many of the same concerns these men had. I wished I could help them see things from my new perspective. But I wasn't sure how to do that at this point, so I took this new passion and became focused on supporting my wife in her efforts.

Beckie and I found new ways to engage with each other to build her business *and* our marriage. We also supported the marriages on her team. We got in the habit of taking her team members and their spouses out to dinner or doing video calls with them, and we'd talk openly and honestly about the role men can (and should) play in their wives' network-marketing businesses. Women kept telling us how much they longed to have their disengaged husbands come off the sidelines and join them in their work.

They shared how they wanted their husbands to support them and how much they wanted to dream *together* with their husbands about what the business could do for their lives.

Too many women never achieve their full potential in network-marketing because of their husbands' lack of support.

The sad reality is that too many women never achieve their full potential in network marketing because of their husbands' lack of support, degrading comments, unwillingness to be involved, inability to understand the business model, and minimizing their accomplishments. I don't know about you, but that's not the kind of husband I want to be.

It doesn't have to be that way. In fact, I've seen dozens of husbands get off the sidelines and support their wives. I've seen them get involved wherever and however they can, becoming their wives' biggest encouragers. The result is a wave of entrepreneurial women who are quickly rising through the ranks of network marketing, changing their families' futures, and truly experiencing the excitement and sense of purpose they hoped for when they started this journey.

After several months of these conversations, hearing both the good and the bad, I could not shake the burden that *someone* needed to write a book to help husbands figure out their place in their wives' businesses. And, if no one else was going to step up to write it, I figured that *someone* had to be me.

WHAT TO EXPECT

My goal in this book isn't just to grow your wife's *business*; I want to help you grow your *marriage*. These aren't separate issues. The more involved you get in her passions and interests and support her in her efforts, the more payoff you'll receive—both in your finances and your relationship. Throughout this book, I'll help you better understand what network marketing is, how it works, and how you can support your wife's business. I'll also help you navigate the often-uncertain waters of talking about her business, challenging her on her goals, and surviving the emotional roller coaster that every network-marketing family goes through. And let's be clear here: I know you probably didn't buy this book for yourself. My guess is that your wife bought it, dropped it in your lap, and asked you to read it . . . *for her*. That's okay. I'm going to make this book as simple and painless as possible for you. I'm sure you are already busy with your own work and commitments, so I can promise that the things we'll talk about in this book won't take a lot of your time. They will, however, make a huge difference for your wife.

The content is broken up into five sections, and each section has five short chapters with a corresponding action step for the day. It's designed for you to read a chapter a day—five days a week—for five weeks, and it will literally take you ten to fifteen minutes a day to get through it. Your wife is spending *a lot* more time than that on her business, right? Hopefully, you can spend fifteen minutes a day to support her.

Section 1: Get Your Head in the Game
First, you have to start by changing your perception of network marketing. Then, you must realize your wife's potential for success in this business, understand the unique challenges of building a business this way, and be able to clarify *why* she's doing it and what winning looks like for your family. This is going to require you to

get your head in the game and change your thinking about network marketing. If you don't, you'll never be able to support your wife effectively.

Section 2: Get Off the Bench

No one ever scored a touchdown from the bench. If you really want to make a difference in your wife's business, you can't stop at simply getting your *head* in the game; you have to get *your whole self* off the bench and make a contribution to the team. Yes, this will require a little time from you, but it's a worthy investment. With just a little time, you'll learn how the business works, figure out your most significant contribution to fuel her success, and be able to set goals together. Her business shouldn't be a solo effort, so put some skin in the game and get involved.

Section 3: It's Game Time

If you're a professional athlete, you're a professional athlete *all the time*. It doesn't matter if you're in the off season, in spring training, or in game four of the World Series; you're always putting in the work to improve. However, each season has its own set of goals and challenges. That's just as true in network marketing as it is in sports. So, if you and your wife want to make the most out of each season, you have to prepare yourself for the rhythms of the business and the different phases of the journey.

Section 4: No One's Undefeated

Every winning team goes through its share of losses. A pitcher may pitch a perfect game here and there. The Dolphins may have had one miraculous undefeated season in 1972. And your wife's business may go through weeks or months of explosive growth. But then, something will happen. She'll lose a critical customer or a business builder. She'll be criticized by people for building a network-marketing business and think about throwing in the towel. You need to plan for those moments as a team. How will you react in tough times? How will you support your wife when she's ready to quit? Losses are coming; it's not a matter of *if* but *when,* so you better prepare for them.

Section 5: Choices That Separate

You know the difference between an ordinary team and an extraordinary team? The answer is right there in the word *extraordinary.* It's that little *extra* you give. The extra effort, extra hours, extra conditioning, extra focus. I have a friend who often says, "Average is average for a reason." He's right. Most people live average, ordinary lives because they aren't willing to do that little *extra* that would put them over the top. If you are willing to make the choices that separate the ordinary from the *extra*ordinary, you will experience an extraordinary life with your wife as you partner with her to find fulfillment and financial success through building her business.

LET'S GET STARTED

If your wife is just getting started in a new business, I'm sure you have a million questions. I know I did at the beginning. We'll cover most of those questions throughout this book, but let me be super clear about one thing right up front. Network marketing is a legitimate business model with the potential for your wife to become wildly successful. But, in order for that to happen, you must do three things. First, you have to be willing to acknowledge any negative impressions you've had of network marketing. We've all seen network marketing done poorly, and that can leave a bad taste in our mouths. I'm going to ask you to set that aside for now and be open to the fact that it *can* be done well. Second, you must admit your skepticism about whether or not your wife can be successful in her new enterprise. There's nothing wrong with healthy skepticism—as long as you use it as fuel to find answers. Third, you must commit to thinking differently about this business model and your wife's involvement in it. If you don't, you'll inevitably hurt your wife, put stress on your marriage, and kill any potential this business has to become a powerful, positive force for your family.

Creating a successful network-marketing business isn't easy. If it was, everyone would be doing it. However, it *is* certainly possible for your wife and your family. Thousands of women are thriving in this business model—many making six figures or more every year. I have the privilege of knowing many of them personally and, of course, I'm married to one myself. I've seen incredible women overcome all kinds of obstacles to achieve things they never thought possible through this business model, and they've changed their families' financial futures in the process. Of all the successful network-marketing women I know who are married, there is one constant: a husband who supported her, encouraged her, fought for her, and, at times, sacrificed for her to achieve the level of success they now experience together. Even if these men were a little late to the game, they eventually showed up and made an impact.

You must commit to thinking differently about this business model and your wife's involvement in it.

That's true in my family, and it can be true in yours, as well. Let's find out how.

SECTION 1

GET YOUR HEAD
IN THE GAME

CHAPTER 1

IT'S LEGIT

IN 1996, I WAS A BROKE COLLEGE FRESHMAN WHEN A GUY IN MY dorm started talking about an incredible business opportunity his parents were involved in. He explained that I could join their team and make a pile of money. All I had to do was convince my family and friends to switch their long-distance phone service to a new company. Oh, and I also needed to recruit some friends to join my team and convince *their* family and friends to switch phone companies. It sounded like easy money, so I signed up right away.

Of course, it wasn't as easy as signing on the dotted line. There was an upfront cost for my startup materials, so, with the full commitment and wisdom of a nineteen-year-old, I put the fee—a few hundred dollars—on my credit card. With that, I was ready to tackle the world of network marketing. Over the next few weeks, I successfully got my parents, grandparents, and about three other people to switch their phone service. And then . . . nothing. Nothing but awkward conversations with friends and a lot of unreturned voice mails. I gave up, writing network marketing off as a con job. I thought network marketers could only be successful by preying on naïve people and becoming master manipulators. No thanks. I turned in my materials, paid off the credit card bill, and said goodbye to network marketing forever—or so I thought.

Flash forward twenty years. My wife, Beckie, got a phone call from some friends who wanted her to join their network-marketing team. And, to my shock and horror, she was getting excited about it. *She can't be serious*, I thought. *These things are scams!* At the time, Beckie was wildly successful in her career, earning more than $100,000 a year as a self-employed blogger and marketing professional. And now she was seriously considering ramping down her primary business and going all in on this

> **How much is this "opportunity" going to cost us?**

new "opportunity" her friends had presented her. I wanted to be a supportive husband, and I knew Beckie was the kind of person who could be successful at anything, but I had serious doubts and a million questions.

HUSBANDS ASK A LOT OF QUESTIONS

Sound familiar? I'm willing to bet you had similar questions and concerns when your wife first mentioned her network-marketing opportunity. Questions like . . .

How Much Money Is This Going to Cost?

You may have some debt you're trying to knock out, or maybe your kids need braces. Most guys have a list of home projects they'd love to take care of, but the money always seems to run out before they can cross them off the to-do list. With so many demands on your money, it's natural to be suspicious of a new business opportunity that comes out of nowhere and promises great earning potential— after the upfront costs, of course. Whenever something like this comes along, our first question is: *How much is this "opportunity" going to cost us?*

How Much Time Is This Going to Take?
Does your family have a lot of free time to spare? For most families—including my own—the answer is "no." People are often as short on time as they are on money, and husbands are quick to ask how much time this new business will take. This is where your wife will explain that a lot of women run their businesses on the side, earning a steady income either on nights and weekends or during the day for stay-at-home moms. She tries to convince you that doing this will give her more energy because she'll be able to pour her passions into something she actually cares about instead of the boring job she's come to hate or spending all day, every day shuttling the kids around between school, sports, and friends' houses. She talks about the sisterhood among the women in the business and stresses that it will meet a social need for her. And she may even pull up an endless stream of video testimonies from women who have invested just ten hours a week into the business and ended up earning six figures, allowing them to quit their full-time jobs. She's really working it, but let's be real ...

Can You Really Make Money Doing This?
Sure, it's great that a few women you've never met have been able to quit their jobs and make real money doing this, but what about *your* wife? Chances are, the lady who told your wife about this business isn't earning six figures at it. Is *she* leaving her full-time job and traveling the world yet? Nope. In fact, you don't personally know anyone who has achieved that level of success in network marketing, so it's hard to believe people actually win at this. Besides, your wife may not have any sales experience, let alone built a sales team from scratch. How can she thrive in a sales-oriented business? Your confidence is waning every minute the discussion drags on.

Does She Really Want to Do This?

You do your best to nip this in the bud, but she's already made up her mind. You've told her that it's probably not as good as she thinks, that it'll be harder than she's expecting, and that most people who fall for a network-marketing opportunity drop out after a few months. She still wants to do it, though, so you give in. *What could it hurt?* you tell yourself. The entry risks are low, so you agree to give it a try. Besides, if momma ain't happy, *nobody's* happy.

So, with excitement, anticipation, and some nervousness, she signs up and starts the network-marketing journey.

IS IT LEGIT?

The first month or two is a bit hectic. She begins using the products and may even force you to, as well. Her nights and weekends are eaten up with training calls, classes, and meetings. She starts stressing out about social media posts and asks you to help her practice the presentation she'll give to customers and potential business builders. Once she starts pitching her product to people in the first couple of weeks, she's discouraged by anyone who says no. Someone might even accuse her of falling for a pyramid scheme or tell her about a friend or family member who had a horrible experience in network marketing. She considers quitting, but her upline rushes in to support and encourage her, so she commits to stay the course.

As a husband, it can be hard watching all this play out. It's a wild roller coaster of emotions with really high highs and really low lows. Every "yes" she gets is a thrill, and every "no" makes her question her whole business. The thing that was supposed to energize her and give her a sense of purpose seems to have left her more stressed than ever before. And what about the money she dreamed about? The first check comes in after a month of long, hard work, and you're shocked to see all that time and effort led to a whopping profit of—wait for it—$103.74. *What?* You do the math and figure out she's been working for $1.15 an hour. You've reached your breaking point on your wife's new business and can't help but wonder, *Is this business model legit?*

Yes, Network Marketing Is a Legitimate Business Model

The Direct Sales Association reports that 5.6 million people are building independent businesses as direct sellers, meaning they are actively managing a customer base and possibly sponsoring others to do the same. Nearly one million of those are working the business full time and earning a full-time income, and nearly three-quarters of them are women.[1] This is, in fact, a legit business model and you *can* make money doing it. However, you have to be careful; there are a lot of bad opportunities out there. It's important to make sure your wife is joining a reputable company with a solid, marketable product and a strong compensation plan that rewards its salesforce. For example, the company my wife works with is a fast-growing, extremely solid, and well-managed network-marketing company. They offer a fantastic consumable product that is truly helping people, and they have nearly one thousand consultants who make six-figure incomes every year. Is every one of their representatives killing it like my wife is? Of course not. But that doesn't mean the potential isn't there. The organization can only provide the product and tools; it's up to your wife to supply the rest to grow her business.

You may argue (or at least quietly believe) that your wife doesn't have what it takes to build a real business. And, the truth is that my wife had already built a successful business before she got involved with network marketing, so she already had a skill set in place. While she hit the six-figure mark much earlier than most, I've met dozens of women who are making that much or more—some who make *seven figures* annually—who started with no business

---

1   Direct Selling Association, "Direct Selling in the United States: 2017 Facts and Data," June 18, 2018, https://www.dsa.org/docs/default-source/research/dsa_2017_factsanddata_2018.pdf.

experience whatsoever. They began their businesses with a dream of building something exciting, they put in the work, and they reaped the rewards. It's not that uncommon. Different studies show that anywhere from 74 to 82 percent of network-marketing professionals are women, and many of them are working hard to do what Beckie has done: work side by side with other women, build long-lasting friendships, earn extra money, and have fun promoting a product they believe in.

Even though network marketing is legitimate, it isn't for everyone. Jon M. Taylor, PhD, conducted comprehensive research and analysis of the compensation plans of more than four hundred network-marketing companies and presented his findings in his e-book, *The Case (for and) Against Multi-level Marketing*. Among his many findings, he reported the staggering dropout rates of network marketers. In the first year of operation, Taylor found a minimum of 50 percent of representatives drop out of the business entirely.[2] It's easy to understand why. The number of hours required to build a business can be intimidating. The stress of talking to friends about your product and opportunity can be overwhelming. And hearing no after no can be demoralizing. Yes, I know a lot of successful network-marketing women, but I've known many more who started with big dreams and then threw in the towel pretty quickly.

> **They began their businesses with a dream of building something exciting, they put in the work, and they reaped the rewards.**

I wonder, though . . . how many of those women who quit their businesses and gave up their dreams in the first year might have

2 Jon M. Taylor, *The Case (for and) Against Multi-level Marketing*, Consumer Awareness Institute, 2001, https://www.ftc.gov/sites/default/files/documents/public_comments/trade-regulation-rule-disclosure-requirements-and-prohibitions-concerning-business-opportunities-ftc.r511993-00017%C2%A0/00017-57317.pdf.

survived if their husbands were a source of encouragement and support during the hard start-up phase? What if the men in their lives had been more patient and had taken the time to build their wives' confidence and comfort level in their business? What if these women, emboldened by their husbands, had busted through the limiting beliefs they had about themselves, taken advantage of the training opportunities around them, and put in the work to build something incredible? Where would they be now? Sadly, this missing 50 percent of business owners will never find out. But your wife can.

What if these women, emboldened by their husbands, had busted through the limiting beliefs they had about themselves.

I'm not saying every woman in the world can and will be successful in network marketing. They won't. But, if your wife is committed to giving it her best and you are committed to actively supporting her, together you have a genuine opportunity to leverage this amazing, *legitimate* business model to see her succeed like never before.

Watching Beckie grow in this business has been incredible. The boost to the family income has been amazing, of course, but the *real* payoff has been the change I've seen in my wife. She's more comfortable, confident, and joyful than she's ever been. She's a better wife, better mom, and better professional since she started her network-marketing business, and I wouldn't trade this experience for anything. That's what I want for you too!

ACTION STEP

Now it's time to put in a little extra effort. At the end of every chapter, I'll give you an action step to put these principles to work in your marriage and in your wife's business. The first action step should be pretty obvious: *read this entire book!* If you're up for it, I want you to tell your wife and one other person that you are committed to seeing this book through to the end. Ask them to hold you accountable and to check in on your progress! This will help you stick with it. And don't take this commitment lightly. Like anything else in your marriage, if you say you're going to do it, *do it!*

CHAPTER 2

SHE CAN

MY FRIEND DREW REALLY *STEPPED IN IT* ... SO TO SPEAK.

His wife, Anna, was a committed mom of three who had built a successful interior design business with her aunt. She was a hard-working, get-after-it kind of woman. Anna enjoyed interior design, but when she was introduced to my wife's business, she got a new vision for what she could do in network marketing. She saw the potential for long-term, residual income as a game changer for her family. Besides, she was already a fan of the product and had some prior experience building a business. So, Anna became a frontline builder working with my wife, Beckie.

Drew, a supportive husband and loving father, was fine with Anna trying out this new business opportunity. He knew she could achieve some level of success, but Anna wouldn't be satisfied with *some level*. From the moment she started the business, Anna set big goals. She knew the first several months of a new network-marketing business were crucial to long-term success, so she committed to creating huge momentum as quickly as possible. That led Anna to a bold declaration in the first week of her business. She declared to Drew, "I'm going to make gold rank, which will enable me to make $3,000–5,000 a month."

Without missing a beat, Drew looked her in the eye and replied, "Right. If you hit gold in this business, I will crap my pants."

That remark, although meant as a joke, stuck firmly in Anna's mind. As supportive as her husband normally was, she realized there was something about network marketing that made him doubt her ability to succeed. She realized he didn't fully believe she could make it in this business—and she was determined to prove him wrong.

Beckie and I weren't surprised later when Anna did, in fact, achieve gold rank. To commemorate the occasion, Beckie had a large package of adult diapers delivered to Drew!

Drew was proud of his wife and a great sport about Beckie's joke, but his comment at the start of Anna's journey revealed something many otherwise supportive and loving husbands do all the time in network marketing: they unintentionally become their wife's biggest limiting belief. If you really want your wife to win in this business, you've got to be on guard against the limitations you accidentally put on her with your thoughtless comments and *innocent* jokes. Let's take a look at a few ways husbands limit their wives' potential and how you can defend your marriage against them.

TYPES OF LIMITING HUSBANDS

I don't think most husbands *intend* to limit or sabotage their wives' businesses. Their limiting beliefs come across more subtly and unintentionally as they question, mock, or passively stew while their wives balance their new businesses with family responsibilities. These women are forced to weigh the encouragement and support they get from their upline sponsors against the indifference or verbal jabs from their husbands.

The truth is, even the best of us struggle with negative, belief-limiting attitudes when we don't fully buy into what our wives are doing. As I've worked with a lot of network-marketing husbands over the past couple of years, I have identified four specific personas that represent who these guys are and how they impact their wives' businesses.

I can generally tell within a few minutes of meeting a couple what role the husband plays in the business. He's either going to be a Passive Pete, Sarcastic Steve, Show-Me-the-Money Matt, or Get-Real Rick. Let's take a look at these, and as we do, be honest with yourself about which one most reflects your attitude toward your wife's business.

Passive Pete

Pete is often frustrated with the amount of time his wife puts into her business. He's kind of lazy—at least with household stuff—and he's gotten comfortable letting his wife handle much of the chores without his help. So, when her new business eats up a chunk of her time, he notices the dropped balls around the house—the laundry left undone, dishes piled in the sink, lack of groceries in the fridge. But he still isn't motivated to jump in and help. Instead, he'll just say, "That's fine," "Whatever," or, "Just do your thing." Inside, though, the frustration is building because he's beginning to realize he's got to step up and help with some things around the house. He feels like his wife's new commitments are creating more work for him and attacking his valuable free time.

> **Even the best of us struggle with negative, belief-limiting attitudes when we don't fully buy into what our wives are doing.**

Passive Pete grows more and more resentful, but he never bothers to verbalize what he's feeling. As a result, a rift starts to form in their marriage, and he begins a cold-shoulder offensive against his wife. Whenever the opportunity arises, Pete will sneak in a passive-aggressive comment about how her business is affecting their family or he'll *jokingly* belittle her efforts—often in front of other people. He'll say things like, "Well, the kids and I don't have clean clothes to wear or anything to eat, but at least she's happy!" Pete is playing the long game, biding his time until his wife gives up her *silly business thing* and their lives can get back to normal.

Sarcastic Steve

Unlike Pete, Sarcastic Steve has no problem voicing his opinion. He is always quick with a joke or, more often, a cutting comment designed to chip away at his wife's commitment to her business. When she adds a new downline team member, he says, "So, you hooked another one, huh? I wonder how long she'll last." When she makes a new sale, he says, "Hey, great job. Really. It only took you four hours to make ten bucks. The money's really rolling in now!" When she gets home from a team meeting, he kills her enthusiasm by saying, "Welcome home from the cult meeting. Did they serve cookies to go with all the Kool-Aid® you're drinking?"

Steve creates a situation where his wife simply cannot win. When she has success, he jumps in to minimize or mock it. When she has a setback, he shines a spotlight on it and uses that painful experience to drive a wedge between her and the business she's trying to build. As a result, Steve's wife is faced with only two options. She can either completely withdraw from him, building her business in secret and being careful not to share this new part of her life with her husband. Or she can give up the business (and maybe her dreams) just to end the torment her snarky husband has been dishing out. Whichever she chooses, one thing is for sure: Sarcastic Steve's marriage has taken a hit, and he's shown his wife a side of himself that she won't forget anytime soon.

Show-Me-the-Money Matt

Unlike Pete and Steve, Show-Me-the-Money Matt is all for his wife's business opportunity—as long as she can make lots of money doing it. But, after the first few months of starting to build her business, Matt gets frustrated. When he realizes she's spent a good bit of money up front to get the ball rolling by attending training sessions or purchasing products, he raises a flag. Then, when he sees the small amount of her first paycheck after all the time and effort she's put into the business, his jaw drops and he is completely done with it.

Matt doesn't care about the relationships his wife is building or whether she's having fun. He can't see the *potential* income, either; he's all about the money here and now. He might even pull out a spreadsheet in the middle of a money fight with his wife, breaking down every dollar going in and coming out of the business. Matt is stuck in the details; he can't see the big picture. All he knows is that his wife has spent several months building a business that so far has only produced a $10 net profit.

Show-Me-the-Money Matt's wife is doomed to fail. She'll never be able to live up to the pressure to get rich quick, and she'll likely skip out on key opportunities for training or development. She'll know Matt won't see those things as investments; he'll see them as wastes of money. She may spend just a few months building the business before giving up—right before her efforts would have started paying off.

Get-Real Rick

Get-Real Rick prides himself on being a realist. He's confident that he has a handle on how the real world works—and this business model doesn't fit into his paradigm. He's convinced it's all a scheme in which a few people at the top make all the money on the backs of the naïve people who do all the work. He uses the term *pyramid scheme* at least ten times a day and jokes about how anyone could fall for such a scam. And now, he's dealing with the fact that his own wife is one of those *naïve people*.

Rick believes the only way to make money is to get a "real job" and work eight hours a day punching a time clock. Side businesses—especially network-marketing opportunities—are nothing but colossal wastes of time and money. He's irritated that his wife is living in la-la land and even more irritated that someone conned her into believing this nonsense. The message that Rick is sending his wife is that her creativity and entrepreneurial spirit don't matter and that her only financial value is tied to the number of hours she's willing to put in working for someone else.

FROM LIMITING BELIEF TO BIGGEST SUPPORTER

These four personas paint a pretty sad picture of what many wives have to deal with in this business. It's not fair to them, and, if we're honest, we know that's not the kind of husbands we want to be. No matter how much of a hardworking powerhouse your wife is, your support and genuine encouragement can and will take her business—and your marriage—to the next level. But how do you shut down the negative voices in your head?

How is my attitude hurting my wife and her business?

First, you need to identify your naturally negative persona. Are you a Passive Pete, a Sarcastic Steve, a Show-Me-the-Money Matt, or a Get-Real Rick? Be honest with yourself. You will remain an obstacle in your wife's business until you admit which one you are and how that attitude is impacting the woman you love. Go back through the four personas and put a big checkmark next to the one that sounds most like you. Ask yourself, *How is my attitude hurting my wife and her business?*

Second, you must take your naturally negative persona out back and shoot it. Make no mistake: your negativity and jokes have an impact on your wife. With every crack or complaint, you are telling her that the business she's building is stupid and belittling something she's grown to care deeply about. Is that how you want to make her feel? How would you react if you heard another guy laughing at her and trying to make her feel dumb? If your negative persona is hurting your wife, you've got to get rid of it for good. Don't let anyone—yourself included—bring that kind of harm and shame on your wife.

Third, you need to change your mindset about this business. Sure, this business has some quirks that are unique to network marketing, but it's nothing your wife can't handle. If you're still wavering on whether you can really trust this business, just hang in there with me. Much of the content in this book will help you better understand how your wife's business works. The more you know, the more comfortable you can be that this is a *real* and *worthwhile* enterprise.

BELIEVE IN HER FIRST

I love the movie *Good Will Hunting*. It's the story of Will, a genius mathematician who struggles to realize his potential. Instead of raising his hand and making a mark on academia, he hides his talents from the world, working as a janitor mopping the halls of MIT. Once others notice and invest in his talents, he finally begins to accept his gifts and trust in his own ability. At a pivotal moment in the film, Will's counselor, played by Robin Williams, observes, "Some people can't believe in themselves until someone else believes in them first." Isn't that what we *all* need at times? When we're facing something hard and scary, we need the people who know us best to give us their support. Our wives deserve that from us. When we believe in them first, we empower them to believe in themselves and trust that they can become successful in their businesses.

"Some people can't believe in themselves until someone else believes in them first."

ACTION STEP

As we wrap up this chapter, I want to ask you a couple of questions. First, are you willing and able to actively believe in your wife? Can you shut down your negative persona, silence the discouraging voices, and trust in her ability to achieve her goals?

Second, if you've been a limitation to her business, are you willing to apologize for any negativity or mocking you've given her since she first mentioned her network-marketing opportunity? She knows what you've been thinking, so apologizing will go a long way toward restoring the trust that may have been lost.

Finally, commit to be a belief-filled, encouraging voice in her life instead of a limitation. She probably *can* build the business without you, but do you really want her to? Why would you *not* want to be involved in something she's so passionate about? Tell her you believe she can do this and that you're committed to supporting her in her success.

CHAPTER 3

CHILL OUT

PAYDAY HAD FINALLY ARRIVED!

Beckie worked her new business for a few months before she ever received a dime of pay. Those were *hard* months. It felt like she was working the business nonstop. I'd estimate she put in more than a hundred hours a month early on to get this thing started—and that was on top of her regular job. Those early days were primarily focused on building the backend of her business by putting systems and processes in place, learning the business model, and recruiting her first five team members (or builders). Then, when she finally had her team in place and officially launched her business, she dove in even harder, working thirty or more hours a week with classes, phone calls, and follow-ups. It was obvious that she had started something great, and I couldn't wait to see how well all that hard work would pay off.

At the end of her first month as a representative, I knew payday was coming soon. I was pumped to get a glimpse of what our family's future might look like. What would we do with this windfall? A vacation? Some home repairs? Reinvest it into the business? There were so many possibilities! I was so proud of all my wife's hard work and couldn't wait to celebrate with her.

Finally, the day came. I fired up my computer and logged into our bank account, ready to welcome the new pile of network-marketing cash into our budget. I clicked through to our daily transactions, scanned the list, and there it was. The deposit I'd been waiting on for months. Beckie's first paycheck from her new business, the business that had dominated so much of her life for the past few months. The income that would free up more of her time, enable her to make money engaging in her passions, and make all our dreams come true. That life of luxury was within reach, and it would all start with this amazing payday of . . . $634?!

I couldn't believe what I was seeing. I stared at the screen, trying to convince myself that the bank had accidentally left a zero off the end of the deposit. I did some quick mental math, accounting for all the hours Beckie had put into the business going back to the first day, and I realized she made somewhere around two bucks an hour for all her efforts. To say it was a huge letdown would be the understatement of the year.

To put that $634 in perspective, Beckie received a check in the mail that same day for $800. However, that $800 wasn't the result of a few months' worth of work, trainings, and phone calls; it was for a single blog post she'd written for a business as part of her regular job. That one post created more income than the hundreds of hours she spent on her network-marketing business. My mind was blown and, to be honest, I wasn't a great sport about it. There was *no way* I'd be okay with Beckie putting in that much effort for a measly two dollars an hour. Her time and skill set were more valuable than that.

IT'S NOT GET RICH QUICK

One of the biggest misconceptions about network marketing is that it's a way to earn a lot of money very quickly and with minimal effort. Sadly, there are a few bad apples in network marketing that actually *promote* their business opportunities that way. Those of us involved in legitimate businesses who have successfully navigated the frustrating first few months of high effort and low reward know that's a lie. There's nothing *quick* about the income you can generate through network marketing. Like I've said before, there is enormous *potential* in this business, but it's not easy or fast for most people. That simple realization is enough to cause many husbands to encourage their wives to quit the business after the first few months. They look at all the time spent on the business—just like I did when Beckie got her first check—and they immediately decide that network marketing isn't worth it. They might as well say, "Well, we didn't get rich in the first few months, so this business must not work. You should just quit."

If you forget the network-marketing aspect and just think of this as building a business, things start to make more sense. Who would expect to jump into a brand-new business tomorrow and have piles of cash rolling in by the end of the first few months? That almost never happens. Instead, the entrepreneur has to walk through a process of building the business. She has to put each piece in the right place and in the right order. That takes time and effort, but it's time and effort no one is paying for. Business owners usually don't make much money while they're laying the groundwork for their business.

There's nothing *quick* about the income you can generate through network marketing.

Think of it this way. The book in your hands is complete. It's been planned, written start to finish, edited, critiqued, typeset, printed, published, distributed, and sold. You, your wife, or someone else paid money to buy this book and, as the author, I'll get a portion of that money as my profit. That's how it works with authors: sell a book, make a profit. It's clean, simple, and relatively quick. Best of all, it requires zero effort on my part for someone to buy a book online or in a store and for someone else to send me a check for my portion of the profit. I can just sit back and smile as those checks roll in.

Here's the thing, though. All that is only true *from your perspective right now*. From where I'm sitting writing this chapter, I'm only two and a half chapters into what I plan to be a twenty-five-chapter book. I've already spent months planning and preparing to write this book. I've had dozens of conversations. I've done research into network marketing. I've outlined the book and individual chapters. I've made plans with my publisher.

Don't expect to get Year Ten results out of a Day One business.

I've researched the marketplace and potential competition. I've started conversations with different organizations for potential distribution deals and bulk orders. I've consulted with an editor. And now, I'm about a week into a writing phase that will last another three months. Altogether, I figure the book you're holding represents about six months of my life. Now, do you know how much money I've made from this book so far and/or will make during these six months of development? Nothing. Zero. Zip. Nada. No book advance money here! I'm spending several nights a week and most weekends working on this, and no one is paying me a dime. At least Beckie had $634 to show for all her hard work after a few months!

Writing a book is a long process, and most of the work happens in private. When most people see a book on a store shelf, they just see a book that's ready for purchase; they don't see the hundreds of hours that were required to bring it to that point. I want you to think of your wife's business like that. You may want to see the finished product and tap into the income she says will come, but it doesn't happen overnight. In those early months, she will spend most of her time putting the pieces of her business together. It's a work in the earliest days of progress, so don't expect to get Year Ten results out of a Day One business.

REFRAME YOUR THINKING

From the time we get our first jobs, maybe around age sixteen, we've been trained to trade time for money. If we work ten hours at $10 per hour, we make $100. It's pretty simple. That time-for-money mentality gets stuck in our thinking, so most of us spend our whole lives trying to earn a higher hourly wage to make the most out of the working hours we have in a day. Or, you might think in terms of selling. If you make something for $10 and sell it for $25, you can keep a sweet $15 profit per unit. Again, it's a simple concept. But this is *not* how your wife will build a successful network-marketing business. If you want to help your wife become successful in her business, you must change your thinking. In the first few months—and maybe throughout her entire network-marketing career—she isn't simply trading her time for money or actively selling a product with a high markup. She's building a machine that will pay off in the long run for her and for your family.

Investing in anything requires a long-term mindset.

For the first several months (or even the first year depending on how quickly she wants to ramp up), your wife will be in the *investing stage*. Keep that word *investing* front and center in your mind. When you invest money, you're putting a little money *into* something up front with the expectation of getting a lot of money *back out* later. When you invest time, you're putting a block of hours into something up front with the expectation of getting a lot of time back later. Investing in anything requires a long-term mindset. You have to trust the payoff will come, but it won't come immediately. In network marketing, this means accepting the fact that your wife will be working many more hours than her paycheck reflects. It will seem unfair at times, and you may think she's being taken advantage of. But she's not. She's *investing*. She's made a decision to invest her time into building something she believes wholeheartedly will pay off later. Give her the space and time to do that.

Once she makes it through the investing stage, she will move into the *trading stage*. This is where things will start to feel more comfortable for you. You'll be able to see a more direct connection between the time she spends working the business and the money she's making for her efforts. This gets back to the familiar time-for-money tradeoff we learned with our first jobs. While it's nice to see such a direct reward for her time, this stage can be a bit of a trap. Sure, she can stay at this level, but, at this point, all she's done is made herself an employee. It isn't a *business* that she *owns*; it's a *job* where she has to *work*. That's not where she needs to stay; if she does, she'll get stuck.

However, if she continues to do things right and follows the plan her upline sponsors have outlined for her, she should move through the trading stage and into the *winning stage*. This is where the magic happens. Here, she isn't simply working on commission or trading time for money. At this stage, she's a full-fledged business owner. She's leading a team of people who are each focused on building their businesses. And, as they build *theirs*, they also help build *hers*. All the activity happening in her downline doesn't require much of her time, but it creates all-new rewards for her. That means she's working less and making more. That's the sweet spot, and it's where you and your wife want her business to go.

THERE IS NO GOLDEN GOOSE

Too many people simply want a money-making machine that sits quietly in the corner and constantly spits out dollar bills. Believe it or not, I'm not going to tell you that's impossible. The truth is, a solid network-marketing business *can* generate a lot of passive income. But—and this is what many husbands overlook—the first step in having a money-making machine is to actually *build the machine*.

A golden goose isn't going to wander into your house and pop out twenty-four-carat comfort all on its own. You've got to invest the time, energy, blood, sweat, and tears into building the business that will ultimately pay off for your family. That's what your wife is trying to do. What she needs from you is your patience and support.

ACTION STEP

The action step for this chapter isn't an action at all. In fact, it's the reverse. As you reflect on this chapter and the first several months of your wife's business, I want you to chill out. Relax. Take it easy. Stop yelling, "Show me the money!" every time you see her working on her business. Give her the time and space she needs to invest in her business and launch it successfully. If you want this to be a fruitful enterprise for your family, back off a little bit. Give it time to establish the firm foundation it needs to survive and thrive over the long haul.

CHAPTER 4

SET A PACE

My wife is a sprinter. She thinks fast, works fast, talks fast, and drives fast. She gets more done in a day than most people do in a week. Combine that with her strong work ethic and leadership abilities, and she is a force to be reckoned with. That makes her an amazing business owner, but it can also make her a little intimidating to new people coming onto her team. One of her earliest team builders saw Beckie's pace and thought about quitting, questioning whether or not she could maintain that pace. Fortunately, her husband was plugged into her business and had a good sense of what she could accomplish. He encouraged her to stick with it, saying, "You hang on to Beckie's coattails and don't let go!" Smart guy. His wife fought through her intimidation and is now a frontline leader on Beckie's team who is making *significant* income.

Sprinting isn't for everyone. Many people would become discouraged and give up if they thought they had to keep the throttle wide open 24/7. The good news is that your wife can choose what speed she wants to use for her business. We'll cover four different speeds in this chapter, and each speed has its own set of challenges and opportunities. In order to have the right mindset to support your wife's business, you'll need to discuss and agree on what speed makes the most sense for her and for your family.

THREE SPEED FACTORS

Before we look at the four speeds, we need to quickly review three key speed factors. These are the things you must know before you and your wife determine how fast (or slow) she wants to grow her business.

First, you must know how your wife is wired. I've said that my wife is a sprinter. It's who she is and who she's always been. No matter what she's done or where she's focused her energies and passions over the years, she goes full force into every opportunity. But that's Beckie; your wife may be the exact opposite. She may prefer to take things slow, carefully weighing every decision as she builds her business one piece at a time. There's no right or wrong way to do it. The goal is to understand how your wife is built and to let that guide your business-building decisions.

Second, you must consider what's best for your current stage of life. Do you have young children? Is your wife working full time? Do either of you travel for work? Are you about to start a family? Are you empty nesters? Does your schedule allow you extra time to work with and support her in the business? Her business will not exist in a vacuum, so you have to take a clear, honest look at your current family situation. Only then can she estimate the best speed for meeting her goals, maintaining her priorities, and keeping her sanity.

Third, you must accept that the faster the speed, the more support she will need from you. If she wants to build her business fast, you'll have to invest more into it and possibly pick up more responsibilities at home. This may be as simple as finding more efficient ways to do things, eliminating wasted time, limiting time spent on hobbies, turning off the TV, or cutting back on social media. Whatever you choose to do, be realistic about the fact that there's a direct connection between how fast she wants to go and how much help she'll need from you.

With these three things in mind, now let's talk about the four speeds your wife can use to build her business.

THE FOUR SPEEDS FOR BUILDING HER BUSINESS

The four speeds are easy to remember, and you should be able to quickly grasp what I mean by each one. The women in these illustrations all built their businesses at their own pace. My hope is that you'll read these stories, discuss them with your wife, identify the right speed for your family, and have the clarity and confidence to move forward together.

Speed 1: Walk

Stacy is a walker. She works full time and has three kids ages seven to thirteen. She chose to invest five to ten hours a week into her business, and she's made slow and steady progress from the start. After a full year, she began to see some momentum. That's when her husband first noticed a *real* paycheck. She remains focused on income-producing activities, personal development, and great customer support, but she's careful not to let

The faster the speed, the more support she will need from you.

the business get away from her. She knows exactly where it fits in her life right now, and she's patiently building it to where she wants it to be.

Walking takes a long-term view. If your wife chooses a walking pace for building her business, you must both commit to a two-year mindset. It will take a lot longer to build momentum, so she will have to be mentally strong when it feels like she's not making much progress. Setting clear and measurable six-month goals will help with this. Even though she's committed to going slow, she still needs to have her sights set on *something*.

Moving at this pace also means there will be long stretches

when nothing seems to happen in her business, and she may be tempted to go weeks at a time without working on the business at all. Encourage her to stay the course! Remind her of her six-month goals and help hold her accountable to a weekly routine of a few income-producing activities.

A walking pace may not be as outwardly impressive as others, but it is extremely sustainable with a low risk of burnout—as long as the business owner understands she's not going to hit the big milestones for a while. To thrive as a walker, your wife must remember that her business will be built brick by brick over a long period of time by a series of small investments. If she's willing to do that—and if you're willing to patiently walk alongside her—she'll eventually walk her way to success.

Speed 2: Jog

Anna is a jogger. She works full time and has three kids between ages eight to fourteen who are involved in sports. She is great at finding customers and loves to attend (and lead) classes a couple of nights a week to learn new ways to engage her customer base and support her growing team. She decided early on to spend ten to twenty hours a week on her business, and that led to steady growth. Now, after sixteen months of building, she has a decision to make: she's either going to take the leap and go full time in her business or she's going to keep her regular job, be content with where her business is, and downshift into a walking pace to maintain what she's built.

Jogging requires a one-year mindset—and you must be prepared for it to be a challenging year. This can be the most frustrating pace for many, because it's an in-between speed. She's moving fast enough to wear herself out from her efforts, but not so fast that she's going to see quick results. The jogging pace is often the only choice many women have if they want to get involved in a network-marketing business. If they're working full time and have families to take care of, they may not have any more time to give the business. They may *want* to pick up the pace, but their real-world limitations simply won't allow it.

Joggers must fight against frustration at their slower pace and longer-term goals. One-year goals are hard to maintain, so she'll want to set short-term goals to help keep her eyes on the prize. Many women in Beckie's business have chosen to motivate themselves with goals that will ultimately give them more time and fulfillment. For example, your wife may set a goal to make enough money in her business to hire a housekeeper to come clean once a week. Or, she may set a financial goal to take a nice vacation with you—maybe even one *without* the kids. Other motivating goals could be making a sizable donation to a charity you both support, paying off debt, or funding some home-improvement projects you've been wanting to do.

Speed 3: Run
Leslie is a runner. She is a highly networked stay-at-home mom who tried several different odd jobs before getting involved in a great network-marketing company. When she saw the growth opportunity of the business, she stormed out of the gates, quickly investing twenty to thirty hours a week into her business. With her husband's support, Leslie was making $2,000 per month within four months. At the ten-month mark, she hit a rank that gave her the ability to make $100,000+ per year. She's continued to run at a fast pace and is building an extremely successful business.

Runners like Leslie operate with a six-month mindset. They're going fast enough that it can be hard to forecast beyond six months out. Leslie, for example, probably didn't expect to be making six figures less than a year into the business, so shorter-term goals worked better for her. That gives her a big goal to work toward and the opportunity to reset and reevaluate a couple of times a year to make sure her growth is staying on track.

If your wife wants to run at this pace, your full buy-in and support will be crucial to her success. This pace will disrupt your life, so be prepared for some chaos. Running is an incredible way to build momentum quickly, but it is not for the faint of heart. The biggest danger for runners—especially early in the business—is burnout around months two or six. At those markers, she could either quit because she's so tired or get complacent in her quick success and begin a gradual business decline as she loses her sense of urgency.

Beckie has several runners on her team, and I've noticed two keys that have allowed them to survive at a runner's pace without going crazy. First, runners must set their sights on their next six-month goal, create a clear plan to get there, and track it monthly. For example, she may set a six-month goal to enroll ninety new customers. To hit that goal, she'll need to enroll at least fifteen new customers per month. That gives her the six-month goal and gives her the measuring stick to use each month to see if she's on track.

Second, runners (and their husbands) need to create intentional imbalance in other areas of their lives. If you've already got a hectic family schedule, there's no way your wife will be able to start investing up to thirty hours a week into a new business without making adjustments elsewhere. Something *has* to give, so you better plan for it. We'll talk more about intentional imbalance in Section 3 of this book.

Running is a fantastic way to get a new business going quickly, but don't let this pace ruin your family. You want your wife's network-marketing business to be a blessing for your family, not a curse!

Speed 4: Sprint
As I said earlier, my wife is a sprinter. She hit a rank that allowed her to make $100,000+ per year in her first four months. By month

sixteen, she achieved a rank that would enable a $300,000+ annual income. Our lives have been radically changed by what she's accomplished in her business, and we are extremely grateful for that. However, it hasn't been without its share of sacrifice. Beckie worked a lot during that first year and a half. I can't even add up the number of hours she spent in classes, on the phone, meeting people, traveling to support her team members, researching product and market trends, and a million other daily tasks that were required to sprint to success. If your wife wants to sprint, you've got to be prepared for your world to be turned upside down for a while as she focuses on the business.

Sprinting requires a three-month mindset. As your wife adds people to her team and begins to rank up in the company, change will be constant every few months and she'll feel like she's always jumping from one fire into another. There will be wild swings from highs to lows and back again, and her level of exhaustion will make the swings even wilder. Yes, the payoff can be *huge*—but so can the toll it takes on her and the entire family. Do not go blindly into this pace without having serious conversations about what sacrifices you are and are not willing to make. This pace is a terrible option for most people, but if you and your wife are up to it and determined to make the biggest bang as quickly as possible, the payoff can be amazing.

GO THE DISTANCE

Do you know what walkers, joggers, runners, and sprinters all have in common? They're all moving in the same direction: *forward*. It's not about how fast your wife builds; the key to success is to go the distance at whatever pace she picks. That's how you win in network marketing! And, if you need to adjust your pace along the way, do it!

ACTION STEP

Ask your wife to read this chapter to better understand the pace concept. Then, have a conversation about what pace she thinks makes the most sense for her and your family. It's her business, so let her lead the conversation, but be ready and willing to jump in and share your honest opinions about what you are and are not willing to do (or give up). She needs to make a wise decision about pace, and she can only do that if she knows exactly where you stand on things. Once you agree on a suitable pace, set a three-month checkpoint for you both to have another conversation to see how things are going and evaluate if this is still the pace that makes the most sense.

CHAPTER 5

THE WIN

My friend Amy knows what winning looks like for her family—but it didn't start out that way. When she married Mike, she dragged $100,000 of student loan debt into the marriage. The couple soon had a baby and the young family found themselves in deep financial trouble. Amy and Mike had no idea how to climb out of the hole they were in. She felt so incredibly guilty for bringing so much debt into their lives, and she was desperate for a way to pay it off and get rid of the burden. That's when my wife approached Amy with her network-marketing opportunity. She instantly saw the earning potential and committed to building this business to pay off the debt that had stolen their financial future and had become a constant source of stress in her marriage.

Amy's win was clear: *pay off the debt.* And she kept a scorecard every month that showed her if she was winning or not. When the debt amount decreased, she knew she was winning. In months when she cut a huge amount of debt off the pile, she knew she was *really* winning. In months when the total debt didn't budge, she knew she needed to up her game. That clear picture of *the win* was a fixed point in her mind. It shaped every business decision, every goal, and practically every thought she had about her business. That vision for victory also brought Amy and Mike closer together. He saw firsthand how committed she was to helping the family get rid of the debt, and he was able to cheer her on and support her business. They could only do this because they had their eyes fixed on *the win*.

WIN VS. WHY NOT

Let's be clear here. Network marketing is a tough business. It's easy to get into and it's fairly easy to make *some* money in, but real success—the kind of success Amy wanted—doesn't happen by accident. It takes a lot of hard work and a serious amount of intentionality. Achieving anything of value, especially when it's hard to accomplish, requires a deep sense of purpose driven by a clearly defined *win*. Your wife's *win* is the foundation for her business; it's her reason for getting into the business in the first place, and it's the thing that will keep her moving forward through the obstacles instead of giving up.

We all know people who started something with big dreams and then gave up as soon as things got difficult. These are the guys who go hard-core on their diet and exercise plan for four days before throwing in the towel with some lame excuse. These people never achieve the things they say they want because they never make their *win* as strong as their *why-not*.

Why-nots are everywhere. They're the million excuses we give for why we can't do something or why this business model won't work. *It takes time we don't have. The outcome is uncertain. It's going to be hard. It will require sacrifice.* Blah, blah, blah. Everyone thinks *their* why-not is unique, that they have problems, stressors, or limitations that no one else has. I'm calling bull. We're all busy, and we can all come up with an endless list of excuses. But what if you and your wife changed that? What if you came together and crafted a clear and compelling picture of what winning looks like for your family? Your *win* would become the true north of your wife's business, and you'd always know if you were winning. But, without a clear and compelling *win* for her business, you'll both keep falling for the why-nots.

CRAFTING YOUR WIN

The best way to figure out your *win* is to identify your *why?* You and your wife need to understand the underlying reason for her involvement in this business. When you know *why* you're doing something, it's a lot easier to know what winning could and should look like.

The idea of discovering your *why* is all the rage in business and leadership books these days. Author and speaker Simon Sinek re-popularized the concept with his 2009 TED Talk, "How Great Leaders Inspire Action," and his 2011 bestselling book, *Start with Why*.[3] However, the basic premise goes back to nineteenth-century Japanese inventor and industrialist Sakichi Toyada, whose son later established the Toyota car manufacturing business. Toyada introduced the concept of the Five Whys into his businesses: whenever a problem happens, ask *why* five times to dig down to the root cause.

Your wife's win is the foundation for her business

For example, if you're faced with a car that won't start, you could run through the Five Whys to figure out the real reason:

1. Why won't the car start? The battery is dead.
2. Why is the battery dead? The alternator is not functioning.
3. Why is the alternator not working? The alternator belt is broken.
4. Why is the belt broken? The alternator belt is well beyond its useful service life and hasn't been replaced.
5. Why hasn't the belt been replaced? The vehicle has not been maintained according to the recommended service schedule.

3   Simon Sinek, *Start with Why* (London: Portfolio, 2009).

So, as you can see, the clear *win* in this scenario would be to keep up with the recommended service schedule; that would have prevented this problem. But, when the car owner is busy or lazy or doesn't want to keep up with the recommended maintenance, he can expect to have problems a few miles down the road. The breakdown may seem to occur out of nowhere, but it's actually the eventual consequence of an earlier bad decision.

Now, how does that play out in your wife's network-marketing business? What can we learn from the Five Whys to help you and your wife create a clear and compelling win? Let's go back to Amy and Mike's story and break down her reasons for getting involved in her business:

1. Why does Amy want to do this business? So she can make extra money.
2. Why does she want to make extra money? She wants to contribute financially to their family.
3. Why does she want to contribute financially? She wants to pay off the $100,000 in student loan debt.
4. Why does she want to pay off the debt? It's a huge source of stress in their marriage.
5. Why is it a huge source of stress in their marriage? Amy feels incredibly guilty about bringing the debt into the marriage and she feels like it's limiting any hope they have at long-term financial security.

If Amy and Mike defined the win as "make extra money," they would have given up the business the first time or two someone said no to Amy's product or opportunity. Fortunately, this couple received great coaching that helped them dig deeper. When they realized the *real* reason for Amy's business—to pay off the debt, freeing herself from guilt and enabling their family to move forward into a more secure future—they were motivated to hang in there when things got tough. That clear picture of winning fueled her efforts and thickened her skin because it showed her what she was really fighting for.

Knowing her *win* is crucial for your wife's business. Without it, her business will likely never grow beyond a passing interest or hobby—one you'll probably encourage her to give up the instant things get tough. Nobody wants to walk into a business that's doomed to fail, so you and your wife will have a chance to identify her *win* in the action step for this chapter. First, though, we need to look at the flip side of the coin....

FIGHTING YOUR WHY-NOTS

Once you and your wife have targeted a clear and compelling *win*, the next step is to identify the most likely why-nots that will attempt to sabotage her efforts. As I said before, a why-not is simply an excuse, a reason we tell ourselves for why we cannot, should not, or will not accomplish something we set out to do. These are all around us, but I've identified three big why-not categories when it comes to network marketing: other opportunities, outside criticism, and internal fears. Let's break these down.

> **A why-not is simply an excuse, a reason we tell ourselves for why we cannot, should not, or will not accomplish something we set out to do.**

Other Opportunities

The first batch of why-nots falls into what I call *other opportunities*. This is basically anytime you or your wife set aside your goal in order to do something—*anything*—else. You'll know you're struggling with this if you find yourself saying things like:

- I don't have enough time to do this right now.
- I deserve to take a week off and enjoy some me-time.

- I *was* going to work on the business today, but I got tied up watching the full slate of football games or sucked into social media and lost track of time.

This is where we surrender our win one distraction at a time. If we want to succeed and reach our goals, we must focus on the thing that's right in front of us. In this case, it's your wife's business.

People who struggle with this why-not always think the grass is greener on the other side of fence. They think someone else has it all figured out and is living the life they want to have for themselves. Do you or your wife struggle with thinking that someone else's grass looks greener? If so, here's a little secret that might help you put things in perspective: the grass is always greener on the side that's being watered. If someone is killing it in this business, it's because they're laser-focused on reaching their goals. They've identified their win and are going after it. That's great for them, but your success won't look like their success. Each person has to clarify what winning looks like for herself. Once you and your wife have that goal in mind, get to work! Get after it, stop getting distracted by other people and other opportunities, and do the work that's required to build your business to accomplish your win.

When you use outside criticism as an excuse to quit, you're handing the power of your win over to someone else.

Outside Criticism

Network marketers have to deal with all kinds of outside criticism. It's easy to let that build up into a wall of why-nots and cause you or your wife to say things like:

- My cousin thinks we're crazy for trying this.
- I wonder if people think we're stupid for believing we can really build a successful business this way.

- If I hear someone say *pyramid scheme* one more time, I'm going to walk away from the business for good.

These are the times when the two of you will need to look at the world around you and yell, "Shut up!"

When you use outside criticism as an excuse to quit, you're handing the power of your win over to someone else. You're letting others decide if your win is worth it and allowing them to direct where and how you spend your time and energy. Don't do this! If you both set your sights on something and feel it's worth your family's commitment, then shut down the outside voices that try to distract and derail you so you can keep your eyes on the prize—the prize that, together, you have identified for your family.

Internal Fears

Network marketing also causes us to face the negative voices inside our own heads. If you or your wife's biggest why-nots are caused by your own internal fears, you'll say things like:

- We can't move forward in this business. We don't have any sales experience, and we hate talking in front of people.
- If we ask a friend to join the business, they'll say "no" and then things will get weird between us.
- We've failed at this kind of thing before. Why should we believe we can do it now?

Internal fears try to convince us that we can't achieve our wins. This results in a constant state of frustration and disappointment because we feel stuck between what we know we want and what we think we can't do. We end up paralyzed.

As long as you allow your internal fears to steal your focus, you'll be like a hamster on a wheel. You can run and run and run, but you'll never get anywhere. You'll distract yourself with all kinds of activity that makes you *feel* like you're working, but you'll be scared to do the real work of getting in front of people and taking risks to move the needle in your business. Success toward your win requires you to get off the treadmill and build real momentum—the kind of momentum that takes you out of your comfort zone and forces you to confront your worst fears about yourself. If you can't do that, you and your wife will simply spend the rest of your lives trading your wins for your fears, and that's a bad deal all the way around.

SECTION 1 WRAP-UP

Before we get to this chapter's action step, let's take a quick look at what we covered in this section. First, we saw that network marketing really is a legitimate business model. Second, I challenged you to accept the fact that your wife really *can* win in this business and encouraged you to come alongside her as her biggest supporter. Third, I told you to chill out for a while and give your wife room to grow her business. Fourth, we reviewed the different paces in networking marketing and I encouraged you and your wife to discuss what pace she wants to use. And now, in this chapter, we discussed the importance of clarifying the *win* for your wife's business.

With this groundwork in place, we're ready to head into Section 2: Get Off the Bench. There, we'll take a closer look at how you—as the awesome, loving, supportive husband that you are—can step in and make a huge difference in your wife's business.

ACTION STEP

Sit down with your wife and, together, identify what winning at this business looks like for your family. Don't rush this, and don't settle for surface-level or obvious answers. Use the Five Whys mentioned in this chapter to dig deeper and get to the real reasons, hopes, and dreams for this business. With her *win* clearly in mind, discuss her most intimidating and prevalent *why-nots*. Write them down and post them where you can both see them each day as a reminder of why she's doing this and what kind of opposition she can expect.

SPOTLIGHT ON SUCCESS

Ernie and Myra Yarbrough
Young Living, Royal Crown Diamond

When my wife, Myra, first signed up with her network-marketing company, she and I agreed that it was only for the products and not for the business opportunity. It's not that we didn't like or trust the business model; it's more that we saw how many people in network marketing defined success. We weren't that motivated by fancy cars and big houses, and we didn't define success in terms of yachts. We just wanted to love and serve people, so we were happy to use the products and ignore the business side—at first, anyway.

Myra was a full-time mom then, fulfilling her long-time goal of homeschooling our children. She started working her network-marketing business on the side, and things started picking up steam. Her paychecks kept going up, and we started to dream about what it'd be like if I didn't have to work at my engineering job. I'd always had dreams I wanted to pursue, but I never had the time. Once we really started looking at her network-marketing business, though, new opportunities began falling into place and we started working it together.

Myra and I sat down one night and asked each other what we could do, pursue, and enjoy if we were financially free. What would life be like if we knew her network-marketing business would always be there to pay our bills without me having to go off to work every day? We asked ourselves what God put us here to do and what things were so deeply rooted in our hearts that we simply *had* to do them if money wasn't an issue. What were the things that, if we pursued them, could change our lives, our family, and maybe even the world around us?

Those conversations changed our lives forever. It was the first time we really dared to dream about actually *doing* the things we felt called to do. It was so liberating! And, as a husband, it was amazing to see my wife blossom like a flower in the sun when she realized this business would let her flourish in her gifts of hospitality and service while also providing an income and the freedom to travel our family had always wanted.

Finding our big win together was the most exciting thing we've done as a family. And now we get to live out that *win* every day!

SECTION 2

GET OFF THE BENCH

CHAPTER 6

IT'S NOT A SOLO SPORT

"LISTEN, HONEY. THIS IS *YOUR* THING; IT ISN'T *OUR* THING. I'VE GOT other things on my plate."

Carla's husband, Eric, had no interest in helping his wife in her business—and he never hesitated to say so. She was a high-energy stay-at-home mom with three kids. Carla loved being home with her children, but she was ready for a challenge. So, when she was presented with the opportunity to build her own business around a product she believed in with a great team of women she enjoyed spending time with, she jumped at the chance. Carla came out of the gate strong. She put her trademark intensity and initiative into her work for the first few months and was on her way to building a profitable network-marketing business for herself. She just needed a little help.

Eric was working a full-time job and had recently started playing around with a side business of his own. He was fine with Carla "doing her thing" as long as it didn't interfere with his life or interrupt his schedule at all. In the first crucial months of her business, Carla found herself hauling her three kids with her to business meetings and workshops because Eric couldn't (well, *wouldn't*) watch the kids. She had little to no time to spend on the business on the weekends because that's when Eric worked on his side gig, and he wasn't willing to cut back his time on that. As the weeks went on, Carla grew increasingly stressed and frustrated as she tried to build a legitimate business with no help from her husband. When she finally sat him down to ask for just a little help, he said "no." He reminded her that it was *her thing*, not *their thing*. After six months of pushing the boulder up the mountain all by herself, Carla had enough and quit, walking away from the strong foundation she'd spent half a year laying.

Carla's business failed because she and Eric approached it like a solo sport. When a runner gets tired, for example, she has no one else to lean on. When a weightlifter struggles to lift the weight on his shoulders, there's no one there to help carry the load. In a solo sport, it all falls on the individual; they win or lose *alone*. Too many husbands approach their wives' network-marketing business like a solo sport. They, like Eric, view it as *her thing* and not *their thing*. This puts these hardworking women in a lonely and discouraging position, and it makes them much less likely to reach their potential. If you want your wife to reach her goals and build a business you can both be proud of, you can't leave her on the field alone. You've got to get out there and find some way to make *her* thing *your* thing.

NEGATIVES OF THE SOLO MENTALITY

Beckie and I have seen this solo-sport mentality a million times as she's grown her business, and it always seems to end the same way. I want to call out three specific negative outcomes of this mentality. These should be huge warning signs for you because they won't only affect your wife's business, but they'll also have a big impact on your marriage—and not in a good way.

She Feels Alone
I'm sure you love your wife; otherwise, you wouldn't even bother reading this book. And, since you love her, I know you

don't want her to feel alone. But here's the harsh truth: if you stay firmly planted on the bench while she's struggling through the ups and downs of building a business, she's going to feel like you've abandoned her to win or lose all by herself. That is such a lonely place to be. Think about it from her perspective. What if you were working your butt off trying to build something and she expressed zero interest? She never offered to help, never asked how things were going, and never gave a word of encouragement when you clearly had a frustrating day. Would you feel loved or supported? Would you feel like your wife was on your team, or would you feel like you were left to figure things out all by yourself?

Building a business—especially a network-marketing business—is hard work. No one should be forced to do it alone.

You Become a Critic

How many times have you been at a football game or watched one on TV when your team was having a rough day? Imagine one of those games where everything that *can* go wrong *does* go wrong—fumbles, incomplete passes, and interceptions. The stands get pretty rowdy during those games, don't they? You can hear *boos* echoing throughout the stadium. Everyone in the stands is quick to stand up and yell at their team. They point out the problems, shout insults at the players on the field, and say things like, "This would never happen if so-and-so were still coaching." Every athlete knows the fans will turn on you at the drop of a dime and, when they do, things get ugly.

Here's the thing about fans: they only show up on game day. The only thing they care about is the win; they aren't interested in what it takes to get there. They expect their team to perform and, when they don't, the fans turn into the biggest critics. I hate to say it, but this is what happens to a lot of husbands who are merely *fans* of their wives' network-marketing businesses. They're happy to see the paychecks coming in (*the win*), but they aren't interested in the work it takes to make that happen. And if the paychecks don't come as quickly as they'd like or as consistently as they'd like, well . . . we already know what happens to fans when their team loses.

Keith Minier, my friend and pastor, often says, "It's easy to be a critic when you're not a contributor." To put it another way, if you don't have any skin in the game, it's easy to sit back and criticize your wife's business. Sadly, that's what most husbands do while their wives work hard to build their businesses alone.

It Creates Division

Do you work hard for your family? I bet you do. My guess is you work long hours trying to build a better life for the people you love most in the world. Maybe you've even gone back to school or worked a ton of overtime trying to get ahead at work to provide even more opportunities for your family. Imagine doing all that, without your wife even noticing. What if she never thanked you for your hard work or supported your efforts? What if she called your overtime hours *your thing* and made it clear that she didn't want it to intrude on her time or schedule at all? That doesn't sound right, does it? I'd actually feel pretty devalued (not to mention angry) if my wife met my hard work with that kind of attitude. After all, I'm doing all this for my family! How can she not see that and at least say *thank you*?

> **"It's easy to be a critic when you're not a contributor."**

Here's the harsh reality: this may be exactly what you're doing to your wife. Chances are, she's building this business for your family, not for herself. She may want to bring in extra money to give your family a little more breathing room or to achieve some big goals you've set together. She's spending her precious free time, her nights and weekends, trying to benefit your family financially. When you call her business *her thing* and insist that it can't interfere with *your thing*, you're putting a wall between you and your wife. And that division will be there for a long time, whether she builds a million-dollar business or quits after six months.

Your wife's business can't be a solo sport. The bottom line is that your wife's business can't be a solo sport. If she's going to reach her potential in business and if you're going to use this as an opportunity to improve not only your family's financial situation but also your marriage, you've got to get out there and join her team. When you do, you'll turn these three big negatives into three huge positives for your marriage.

POSITIVES OF BECOMING A TEAM

When you're on the team together, the entire dynamic changes. You both feel the pressure to succeed, the thrill of victory, and the sting of defeat. She knows she can lean on you for support and encouragement when she is struggling, and you know you can give her a boost when things are hard. Attacking her business as a team breathes new life into your wife's efforts and puts her at a much greater advantage to reach her potential and achieve the results you both want to see in her business.

The three negatives of the solo mentality we discussed above are toxic, not only for your wife's business but also for your relationship. The good news is that you can flip every one of those negatives into a huge positive by changing your mindset from *solo sport* to *team sport*. The benefits that will come into play when you see yourself as part of your wife's team are huge. Let's dig into some of the positive outcomes now.

She Feels Supported, Not Alone

We all want to feel like our work matters, and we all want to know the people we love the most are in our corner and support our dreams. One of the greatest ways you can make this shift with your wife's business is to start treating *her* wins like they are *your* wins. When you have a big win at work, how would you want your wife to respond? You'd probably want to celebrate! Maybe you'd have a nice dinner, and you'd light up when your wife told you how proud she was of you for the big step you'd made in your career. Guess what? She wants the same thing! Imagine how energized and encouraged she would be if you took her out to celebrate every time she moved up a rank. That simple act would make her feel valued and show her that you really see how hard she's working. The result would be a stronger connection in your marriage and more momentum for her business.

You Become a Contributor, Not a Critic

We already saw how the people in the stands act when their favorite team is having a bad game. But what about the other players on the team? Do they *boo* and laugh? Do they criticize every mistake and missed opportunity? No! They relate because they know how hard the game is. They put their arms around the other players, offering encouragement and support. They do that because they aren't merely *fans*; they're *teammates*. They have

> **Start treating her wins like they are your wins.**

skin in the game, too, so they look for ways to help solve the problems. When you join your wife in her business instead of writing it off as *her thing*, you stop being a critic and start being a contributor because you now understand that you're on the same team.

It Creates Unity, Not Division

Author and pastor Andy Stanley says, "Visions thrive in an environment of unity; they die in an environment of division."[4] When there's unity, the team functions better and wins more often. The same is true when you see yourself as part of your wife's team. When you're truly teammates in the business, you stop trying to manipulate the circumstances to further your own agenda and you reject the notion that her business shouldn't interfere with your life. You realize that you're in this *together* and that teamwork will lead you toward your agreed-upon wins. You also choose to believe the best about your wife and her intentions and actions because you are united in what you're trying to accomplish. That spirit of unity has the power to make or break any team, including yours.

IF YOU'RE THE PROBLEM, YOU'RE THE SOLUTION

Author and speaker Dave Ramsey often says that realizing *you're* the problem is actually good news. If you're the problem, he explains, that means you're also the solution. All it takes is a new decision and a change of direction. If your wife's business is struggling because you've left her to do it all alone, that's a problem you can—and should—fix *today*. Decide right now to change your attitude and be part of the solution and success of your wife's business.

---

4   Andy Stanley, *Visioneering* (New York: Multnomah, 1999), 168.

ACTION STEP

The action step for this chapter is pretty simple, but it can make a powerful difference in your wife's business if you do it (and *mean* it). Type the following into a document:

> *My wife will not have to build this business alone. I will support her with my help, time, and attention. I will get hands-on when she needs me to play a more active role and hands-off if she asks me to back off. I will fully support her as an active, participating teammate as we work to build this business together.*

Leave a space at the end of the document for your signature and today's date. Then, share your commitment with your wife and give her permission to hold you accountable for following through with it.

CHAPTER 7

SHOW ME THE MONEY

ANGELA SCREWED UP. SHE WAS A FEW MONTHS INTO HER NEW BUSI-ness and had started to build momentum. She had recruited a few other business builders to start building out her new team, and a huge company-sponsored product promotion had resulted in Angela's biggest month yet with much more volume than she expected. As she sat to close out the month, she was a little confused about how to write up and organize the extra volume. She knew she wasn't great with numbers and honestly didn't understand the ins and outs of the company's compensation structure, but she didn't ask anyone for help. Instead, she made some assumptions, slotted the sales, builders, and volume where she assumed they should go in her organization, and submitted everything to the company.

Her topline leader reviewed her work after Angela turned it all in and realized that she hadn't made the most of her compensation structure. In fact, if Angela had slotted her sales a little differently, she would have been eligible for a $500 bonus that month! Sadly, it was too late. Angela lost out on that bonus because she hadn't put the extra volume in the best place. When her husband, Eric, found out, he was ticked. As a young couple living paycheck to paycheck with two small kids, that $500 was a painful missed opportunity.

Angela was embarrassed and frustrated. She knew she made

a mistake, but she was also annoyed that Eric was making her feel worse about it. He knew she was struggling to fully understand the nuances of the compensation structure; she told him so herself weeks earlier. He was a numbers guy, but he never offered to help her sort it out. So, who's to blame for missing out on the $500 bonus? Ultimately, it was Angela's business and her responsibility, but Eric isn't totally off the hook here. If he had taken the time to understand the compensation plan and help Angela close out the month, he probably would have spotted her mistake pretty quickly. However, since he left her to figure it out on her own—even after she asked for help—they both missed out on what could have been a big boost for their family.

THE RULES OF THE GAME

Whenever I think about husbands looking at their wives' network-marketing compensation plans, I picture the iconic "Show me the money!" scene in the movie *Jerry Maguire*. Tom Cruise's character, Jerry, is dealing with a high-maintenance sports-star client, Rod, played by Cuba Gooding Jr. All Rod cares about is the money. He doesn't want to hear explanations or excuses; he just wants Jerry to "show [him] the money." After being forced to scream "Show me the money!" a dozen times into the phone, the scene ends with Jerry throwing the phone across the room, more frustrated than ever. Rod, however, laughs and goes on with his day.

As funny as the scene is, I've seen it play out several times in real life—except no one's laughing. A lot of network-marketing husbands act like Rod and they treat their wives like Jerry. They don't want to be involved. They don't want to understand the business. They don't want to study the compensation plan. They just want their wives to show them the money. They put unbelievable pressure on their wives to prove the business works by squeezing every penny out of the comp plan without lifting a finger to help them sort it all out. That's a bad plan. Remember, this is likely a brand-new business model that you and your wife aren't familiar with. As we've seen before, we aren't trading time for money in network marketing. Instead, we're getting in the weeds and understanding how to make the most of the different levels, bonuses, and opportunities in your wife's business. You can only do that when you take a little time to learn the rules of the game and then put them to work for your family.

CONSEQUENCES OF BEING HANDS-OFF

If you take a hands-off approach to this important piece of your wife's business, it will never grow to achieve the win you and your wife have set. I can't be any clearer than that. Of course, I'm not saying your wife can't figure this stuff out on her own; in fact, she may be ten times better at numbers than you are. What I *am* saying, though, is that she needs your input. If you want to set and reach goals together, she needs to bounce ideas off you and have you double-check her work. Each partner brings something unique into a marriage (and a business). To do this thing together, then, you've actually got to *do this thing together*! If you don't, you'll miss out on more than an occasional $500 bonus. I've learned from experience that leaving her to figure everything out alone sets you up for several devastating consequences. Let's run through some of the worst ones.

Each partner brings something unique into a marriage (and a business).

You'll Make Stupid, Costly Decisions

Abraham Lincoln famously said, "If I had eight hours to chop down a tree, I would spend six of those hours sharpening my axe." This is a great reminder that rushing into something without taking the time to prepare practically guarantees failure. In network marketing, a big part of that preparation is understanding the compensation structure. You and your wife should never rush into this business without understanding how to maximize the comp plan. This only leads to problems and missed opportunities. Plus, you'll always be frustrated that the business is underperforming or that you and your wife are making costly mistakes. Beckie and I have seen far too many people miss out on piles of money because they didn't take the time to really understand the structure and they failed to ask questions. If you and your wife go into this blindly, you'll miss out too.

You'll Argue...a Lot

Let's face it: we husbands think we have a lot of good ideas. And, to be honest, we *do* have some gems every now and then. You might even enjoy giving your wife some insights on what she should do in her business. That's great! I'm glad you're getting involved. There's a problem, though. If you don't take the time to understand her compensation structure, your ideas could do more harm than good. You could lead her down some roads that work against the comp plan. Your questions could be harmful too. You might see her making a move in her organization and ask, "Why are you doing that?" Then she'll have to stop what she's doing and defend her decision to you. That could be easily avoided if you would simply spend some time understanding how the business works.

Misunderstanding is at the heart of most disagreements and arguments in a marriage. Throw a detailed, often-complicating compensation plan into the mix, and things only get more confusing. If you don't invest any time studying the plan, don't try to offer her business-building advice. Trust me, it won't go well. She'll either do what you suggest and fail because your information was off base, or she'll do something else (because she knows better) and then have to defend her decision to you. Disagreements without the necessary information lead to arguments every time. But, when you both know the rules of the game, you can have good, fruitful discussions that ultimately improve the business.

You Won't Know How to Achieve Your Win

How do you expect to achieve the win you've both identified if you don't know how to build the business in a way that'll get you there? That's like trying to score a touchdown without knowing where the end zone is! You'll just run in circles until you get frustrated and give up. However, once you understand the rank system, you will both be able to map out a plan to get her where she needs to be to achieve her goals. You'll have clarity on how many other business builders she needs, where she should put them in her organization, how much sales volume she and her downline need, and so on.

Disagreements without the necessary information lead to arguments every time.

EVERY BUSINESS IS DIFFERENT

There's no one-size-fits-all in network marketing. Every company works a little differently with different ranks, bonuses, organizations, and commissions. Some businesses compensate more based on the number of business builders you have. Some are primarily driven by direct sales. Some are a hybrid of the two. Some are set up in an entirely different way. In order for your wife to maximize her specific company's plan, you and she need to understand all the little nuances.

Think of it like buying a new phone. The phone in your pocket is more powerful than the average desktop computer was just a few years ago. These devices we take for granted can do almost anything a high-powered supercomputer can do—if we learn how to use them. Users who dig in, research best practices, and study how-to videos on YouTube can work magic with their devices. People who simply pull it out of the box and only use it for texting and phone calls never realize its full potential. Your wife's business is the same way. If you actually learn how to *use* the business, it can and will become a powerful force in your hands.

This book isn't designed to teach you the ins and outs of every network-marketing company. However, as you and your wife begin this journey, I can give you three key principles to use as you evaluate her specific company's compensation plan.

Make Sure It's a Good Compensation Structure

I've researched several different network-marketing companies' compensation plans. Trust me, they are not all created equal. In fact, many of them are train wrecks that should be avoided at all costs. If your wife is trying to build a business with a company that has a fundamentally flawed compensation plan, get out now! Also, if it's a business built around a product she doesn't personally use and/or believe in, she'll never be satisfied with her business no matter what level of success she reaches. Don't invest your time and energy into something she can't get excited about or will never compensate her appropriately. There are simply too many other fantastic options out there to waste your time on a bad one.

Keep It Simple (But Know the Nuances)

You don't have to get the equivalent of an MBA in your wife's business plan, but you do need to research it enough to know the fundamental systems, processes, and organization of a healthy business. You should know how to achieve different ranks, what the average income is at each rank, and what challenges business owners have to overcome to reach each rank. You should also know how bonuses work and what is required to get them. Understanding how to place business builders in your wife's downline is key, too, because that's often how network-marketing businesses thrive. Read through all the documentation and talk to your wife's leaders to get a handle on the essentials for building a strong business, and then work with her to create and stick to a clear and simple strategy for hitting her goals.

Structure Your Business Around Your Win

Do not get distracted by short-term success. The key in network marketing is to think long term. That's why we spent time early on in this book talking about the *win*, the thing you and your wife most want to get out of this business. If your win is something simple, like an extra $200 a month by working a few hours a week, you'll likely set up the business differently than if she wants to make $10,000 a month working full time. You're playing the long game here, so make decisions today that will get you where you want to be a year from now. We'll talk more about this in a later chapter when we work on team goals.

Make decisions today that will get you where you want to be a year from now.

GET INVOLVED

There's a Chinese proverb that goes something like, "Tell me, and I'll forget. Show me, and I'll remember. Involve me, and I'll understand." Your goal is to *understand* how your wife's business works, and that only happens when you get involved. There's nothing wrong with wanting to see a good payday, but make sure you're doing your part by investing some time into understanding the compensation plan.

ACTION STEP

Ask your wife to set up a meeting or phone call for you with a member of her upline this week. Have that leader walk you (and your wife if she wants a refresher) through the company's compensation plan and ask any questions you need to ask to truly get your head around this business.

CHAPTER 8

YOUR SWEET SPOT

EARLY IN BECKIE'S BUSINESS, I WASN'T EXACTLY SURE WHAT MY role was supposed to be. In my "regular job," I'm a full-time executive pastor of a large church. That means I'm the guy who's responsible for the church's growth strategies, staff management, volunteer training, and community work. Basically, I lead big, complicated projects and organize large teams of employees and volunteers. So, when Beckie started talking to me about her business, several questions popped up, such as:

- What am I supposed to contribute?
- Should I simply support her, or is there other work I should be doing?
- Does she really want my opinion?
- Does she really need me here, or does she think she's doing me a favor by including me?
- What unique value do I bring to the business?
- Does she even want the value I may be able to contribute?

As I've mentioned, Beckie was already a proven entrepreneur when she first got started in network marketing. I knew I had a lot to offer, too; I just wasn't sure what kind of help—if any—she wanted from me. We had to figure out my sweet spot in her business.

WHICH GUY ARE YOU?

You may be exactly where I was in those early days, unsure of what role you can or should play in your wife's business. As I've talked with dozens of guys about this very issue, I've found that many men tend to fall into one of two extremes. They either become the *I got this* guy, convinced that he could revolutionize his wife's business and grow it faster than she ever imagined—if she only listened to what he had to say. Or, they take the opposite approach and become the *I'm out* guy who is immediately overwhelmed by the new potential responsibilities and throws in the towel before he ever gets started. News flash: neither of these approaches will work! Let's look at why.

The "I Got This" Guy

Several months ago, Beckie met with a new friend, Stacy, about joining her team and starting a business. Stacy was excited to get started, and she was even more excited that her husband, Rick, wanted to be involved. Rick had an extensive sales background, and Stacy went on and on to Beckie about the high-level sales training her husband had. She just knew Rick would be a powerful force in her business and help her build faster than others. Well, she was partly right. Rick *was* a powerful force; he constantly pressured Stacy to have every conversation, teach every class, and close every sale *his way*. He set aside Stacy's ideas and even discounted the training materials the company provided new business owners. Whenever Stacy mentioned a different method than what Rick wanted her to do, he got frustrated and said, "Fine. Do it your own way." Before long, Rick's passion faded and he quit the team, leaving Stacy to operate the business as a solo sport.

Within a year, Stacy had built great momentum with her business and was making more than $2,000 per month working the business only part time. This got Rick's attention again. As she rose through the ranks, Rick jumped back in the game and had all-new ideas for getting Stacy to the next level. However, all his ideas were radically different than the proven system Stacy had used to get where she was. They argued about methods and, once again, Rick got frustrated that she wouldn't run her business his way. Even though Rick could have been a huge help to Stacy's business, his refusal to accept any other sales methods caused him to be more of an obstacle than a help to her and left her to continue building her business alone.

The *I got this* guy has a lot to offer, but he will quickly bail if things don't go exactly according to his plan. You may be an *I got this* guy if you:

- Want her to follow your advice to the letter despite the training she's getting from the company.
- Think she should value your opinion more than those who have already built successful network-marketing businesses.
- Don't want to learn new methods because you think you've already got everything figured out.
- Tend to push your wife faster than she feels comfortable moving.

If any (or all) of these things are true of you, you're in danger. There's a good chance you'll get frustrated and quit the team if your wife doesn't follow your instructions to the letter and/or see big results quickly.

The "I'm Out" Guy

Steve loved the idea of his wife, Jackie, building a business. He hated his job, and the young couple saw this as a chance for them to build a business that gave them the financial security they needed for him to quit his job for good. Jackie wanted to do the business together, but Steve resisted. He said, "Look, I'd love for this to enable me to quit my job, but I'm not interested in working the business. Besides, this is for women, right? What could I do to help?" Steve thought he was already doing his part by watching the kids while Jackie taught classes and gave product demonstrations.

As Jackie gained some momentum, she kept trying to pull Steve into the business. She was frustrated that he was leaving her to do this by herself, and he was irritated that she wouldn't leave him alone about it. He didn't see that he had anything to offer the business, so he was content to let this be *her thing*.

You may be an *I'm out* guy if you:

- Feel overwhelmed at the thought of working the business on top of everything else you have going on.
- Are scared this will take more time and energy than you're willing to give.
- Constantly refer to her business as *her thing*.
- Think it's unfair for her to expect you to help.
- Doubt you have anything of value to offer.

The *I'm out* guy is no help to anyone. If you recognize some of these signs, it's time to wake up and realize you may be the thing that's keeping your wife's business from taking off.

FINDING YOUR TOP TWO CONTRIBUTIONS

You've got to contribute *something* to your wife's business. If you don't, it will never grow as big as she wants or achieve your ultimate win. But don't worry; I'm not saying you have to contribute a hundred things or even a dozen things. Just pick two. Find *two things*—two unique contributions—you can bring into the business. If you want to do more and your wife wants you to do more, go for it! You don't want to take over her business, but you should feel free to do as much as you and she want you to do. I believe two is enough to put some skin in the game and show your wife you're part of the deal, but not so much that it should feel intimidating to you or make her worry about you taking over. Besides, I'm sure you're already pretty busy yourself, so keeping it to two things will prevent it from eating up too much of your time.

Your two key contributions will become your sweet spot. But how do you determine what those two things should be? It's as easy as answering three simple questions.

Question 1: What Would You Enjoy Doing?

Think in broad strokes about what you enjoy doing that may translate into a useful contribution to your wife's business. These should be things that give you energy and feel fun. Identifying what energizes you and eliminating what drains you are a great start to figuring out your sweet spot on the team. Some examples might be talking to people about the business opportunity, organizing logistics, keeping up with the financials, working on strategy, or leading the marketing. Write these things down.

> **Find two things—two unique contributions—you can bring into the business.**

Question 2: What Are You Good At?

Now that you know what you enjoy doing, it's time to honestly ask yourself, *Which of those things do I do really, really well?* What comes naturally to you? What kind of work do others trust you to handle, knowing you'll knock it out of the park? This alignment between what you enjoy and what you're good at shows you where your sweet spot can be in the business. Examples may include accounting, closing a sale, teaching a class, training new team members, and encouraging people. Write these things down in a separate list beside the list of things you enjoy.

Question 3: What Are Her Weaknesses?

Okay, now it's time to see how the things you enjoy and excel at line up with your wife's weaknesses. Yes, it's okay to admit your wife has some weaknesses! You're not a bad husband to honestly take note of where your wife could use a little help. Make a third list, this time noting what your wife doesn't do well—or at least as well as she'd like. This could include things like public speaking, paperwork, calendaring, accounting, and any other part of running her business.

Find Alignment

At this point, you've got three lists written down. Now it's time to find points of alignment between them. Your ideal situation is to find a couple of things that you enjoy doing, that you do well, and that your wife *doesn't* do well. If two or three of these things immediately jump off the page, great! You've just identified your sweet spot. If not, go back through the three lists again and look for more general themes. While specific tasks may not rise to the surface, you may at least spot a few areas that you and your wife could explore. (Can you take a wild guess at what the action step for this chapter is going to be?) I've walked many guys through this process and I promise, if you just spend a few minutes thinking through it, you'll find your sweet spot.

Articulate Your Sweet Spot Activities

Once you've identified your top two areas of contribution, articulate a specific, measurable activity that puts those areas into action. Use the same format as the two examples below:

- **Contribution:** Research new ways for my wife to invest in her team.
- **Application:** I will spend two hours a week reading, listening to podcasts, or having conversations about team leadership. I will share my weekly insights with my wife over dinner every Friday night.
- **Contribution:** Handle the accounting side of the business.
- **Application:** I will spend time each Saturday balancing her

accounting (orders, inventory, income, etc.) and provide a monthly summary for us to discuss at the start of each month.

Remember, your insights about your sweet spot won't move the needle at all unless you actually put them to work in the business. So don't stop at just figuring out the areas you can help with; go the extra mile by turning those areas into actions—and then *do them!*

THE RIGHT TEAMMATE

Many men struggle with whether or not they're the *perfect* teammate for their wife in their business. If that's you, let me help you answer the question: *no.* No, you are not the perfect teammate for your wife's business, but you are the *right* teammate. You're her husband, her partner for life. You don't get everything perfect in your marriage, and you won't get everything perfect in her business. That's okay! Your support alone will mean the world to your wife. And the fact that you're willing to invest in this and committed to offering your sweet spot activities makes you the best teammate she could have. Besides, we have to remember that, at the end of the day, this is still *her* business. She should always be more committed to the business than you are, and she should always work harder at the business than you do. You don't have to have equal effort, but you should strive to have equal commitment to the win.

> **You don't have to have equal effort, but you should strive to have equal commitment to the win.**

ACTION STEP

There are two action steps for this chapter. First, you're actually going to do the work we walked through. You really need to write out the three lists and articulate your unique contributions just like I laid out. Second, you should share your sweet spot contributions with your wife, show her how you came up with them, and ask for her permission to apply them toward her business. It's great that you want to help her, but don't butt in where she doesn't need or want your help. If she agrees with where and how you want to help, go for it! If she doesn't, work through the process again with her and discuss ways you can truly join her team.

CHAPTER 9

TEAM GOALS

BECKIE AND I ARE GOAL NERDS. IN FACT, I'D SAY OUR SHARED LOVE of setting and working toward goals is one of the strongest things about our relationship. We set goals for everything—our marriage, raising our kids, our careers, our spiritual growth, our finances, and even our time off. We have goals for places we want to visit and things we want to experience in our lifetime, and we have goals for things we specifically want to do while our children are still at home with us. We love goals!

So, when Beckie started her business, it was natural for us to have a conversation about her goals. We talked about how quickly she would advance through the ranks, how much time she would invest into the business, how many people she would invite to join her business every month, how many follow-up conversations she would have with potential customers and business builders, and, of course, what kind of income she wanted to make for all her efforts. We knew she wouldn't stumble into success; it would only come by her setting and achieving high-quality goals.

When Beckie and I started meeting together with other couples and business builders, I just assumed they would be like us. After all, goals came so naturally to Beckie and me, and we relied on them to take us where we wanted to go. Didn't everybody? Nope. I was actually shocked to learn how few of these women had *any* conversations at all with their husbands about their business goals. It was depressing, really. I realized this one issue was a key factor in why so many husbands are completely disengaged from their wives' businesses. They simply have no idea what she is trying to accomplish and what her plan is to make it happen.

At this point in the book, you've gotten your head in the game, worked with your wife to identify your win, gotten off the bench, committed to being on the team, and started to figure out your role. That's great, but it all falls apart if you're missing one crucial part of the game: the scoreboard.

YOU NEED A SCOREBOARD

Can you imagine how frustrating it would be to go to a professional basketball game that didn't have a scoreboard hovering over center court? You'd have no idea who was ahead or by how much, how much time was left in the game, how many timeouts each team had, or even what quarter it was. You'd sit there watching two teams run back and forth for who knows how long, and then, out of nowhere, you'd hear the ref blow his whistle and the game would be over. Even if they did announce a winner, the victory would feel hollow to you. Not having the score in front of you and a timer counting down would remove every ounce of suspense, anticipation, and excitement from the game. It would be pointless without a scoreboard.

I want you to think about your goals like a scoreboard. In sports, a scoreboard does a lot more than keep a running point tally. It accomplishes three critical things:

1. **Scoreboards keep you engaged.** When you know the real-time game stats, you know how to measure the game and track each team's progress.

2. **Scoreboards keep everyone on the same page.** There's no mystery or secrets in a basketball game when everyone has equal access to the time, quarter, timeouts, and score.
3. **Scoreboards keep you motivated.** Fans and players depend on the scoreboard for motivation. When your team is winning, you can celebrate; when you fall behind, you can react quickly. Coaches would never know when they need to call timeout and draw up a play if they didn't know they were behind in the final seconds of the game.

In the same way, the goals you and your wife set will serve as the scoreboard for her network-marketing business.

Too often, I've seen couples identify their win and then stop. They think it's enough to simply know their win, their ultimate goal, and they fail to set any other specific goals. That's a huge mistake. The truth is, it will take a long time for most of us to achieve the big wins we've set for ourselves. Without smaller goals to act as mile markers, it's easy to get discouraged or burn out while chasing the long-term win that still feels far out in the distance. We can get overwhelmed by how little progress we appear to be making when the only goal we've set is one that will take years to accomplish. We need to break that big win down into smaller goals to help track our progress. Those team goals will be your scoreboard, the tool you'll use to stay engaged, on the same page, and motivated over the long haul.

THE BENEFITS OF GOALS

I once heard someone say that building a business without clear goals is like an octopus on roller skates: there's a whole lot of movement—but no progress! Clear goals that you agree on together, though, will ensure all that activity pays off for you. And, if they aren't, you'll know immediately because you'll be regularly checking the scoreboard. There are countless benefits to setting goals in your wife's business, but I want to call out the three main benefits that I've noticed in our family.

Goals Clarify Our Priorities

When a football team takes the field, they don't run out there without a plan. They know the big goal for the day is to win the game, but they also have smaller goals for total yards, completions, first downs, tackles, blocks, and touchdowns. Those are priority issues for a football player, and he is always making sure his activity on the field is directed at those priorities. Those small goals eventually take the team to their big goal of winning the game. Your wife's business works the same way. Her goals clarify her priorities, and those priorities should determine her activity. And, of course, the only way you can support her is if you know what those goals and priorities are.

> **Building a business without clear goals is like an octopus on roller skates: there's a whole lot of movement— but no progress!**

Goals Maintain Our Focus

I had two flies buzzing around my kitchen the other day. They were together on the window for a while, then they moved to the light fixture, and then they zipped around near the sink. Sometimes they were together and sometimes they were on opposite ends of the room. When I finally had enough, I grabbed a magazine and started swatting at them both. At first, I was just slinging the magazine back and forth in their general direction hoping to get lucky. I wasn't targeting either one of them specifically; I was trying to hit both of them—unsuccessfully, I might add. It wasn't until I gave up trying to get them both and focused on only one at a time that I managed to hit them. Focus was the key. In the same way, you and your wife will have a frustrating time if you're chasing two goals at the same time.

Instead, identify the main goals for her business, prioritize them so you know which one to do first, and get to work on one at a time. This keeps you focused on the right thing at the right time, and it keeps you from being pulled in two different directions and getting distracted by other things that ultimately don't matter.

Goals Drive Togetherness

One of the main reasons Beckie and I are so in sync in many areas of our lives is because we have created clear goals that we agree on and are committed to accomplishing. This makes it easy for me to sacrifice for her and for her to do the same for me. It ensures we are rowing the family boat in the same direction instead of fighting against each other with competing priorities.

CREATING CAM GOALS

If you're new to goal-setting, let me take some of the fear and intimidation out of it. Goals don't have to be super complicated; in fact, they work a lot better when they're not. To keep your goals from becoming an impossible, intimidating burden on your business and marriage, start by creating a few simple CAM goals—goals that are *clear*, *attainable*, and *measurable*. Let's break that down a bit.

Goals Must Be Clear

Goals can't be vague; they should be crystal clear and specific. A good goal gives you an unmistakable target to aim for. For example, if your wife wants to improve her business recruitment, she might set a goal that says, "I will do better at recruiting." That's not a *goal*; it's a *wish*. It's not clear or helpful, and it won't get her where she wants to be. Instead, a better, clearer way to phrase it would be, "I will recruit three new business builders by the end of the month." This leaves no room for ambiguity and creates a clear data point for the scoreboard.

Goals Must Be Attainable

If you set goals you could never reach, you'll constantly set yourself up for frustration, disappointment, and failure. Sure, recruiting fifteen business builders in a month sounds great, but it probably won't happen. Even if your wife moved mountains and managed to recruit a record-breaking nine builders in a month, she'd still feel like a failure because she missed her goal.

Think of goals like stretching. You want it to hurt a little, but you still want to be able to get through the stretch without pulling a hamstring. That kind of goal is attainable—meaning it's within reason—but it's still a bit uncomfortable. It causes you to stay focused and actually work toward your goal because you know it requires some serious effort. Then, when you achieve that stretch goal, you have more confidence to bump your next goal up just a little bit. As you grow over time, you find that you're able to accomplish more in the same amount of time, and your goals can grow right along with you. What's *attainable* today isn't what will be attainable a year from now, so always stretch yourself an inch further than you think you can go.

Goals can't be vague; they should be crystal clear and specific.

Goals Must Be Measurable

Nobody wins a race without a finish line. With goals, that means you have to set a measurable outcome with a specific time frame. That's the only way to know if you actually accomplish your goal. A goal can be clear and attainable, but it will still be a bad goal if you don't apply some measurement to it. For example, you might say, "I will spend more time listening to podcasts about network-marketing recruitment." Sorry, but that's a bad goal. Why? There's no measurement! How will you know if you accomplish that goal? What does "more time" even mean? Is five minutes enough? The ambiguity will wreck your success before you even start.

Instead, you could say, "I will spend two hours a week listening to podcasts about recruitment. I'll take notes as I listen, and I'll share those notes with my team members every Friday." That gives you several points of measurement: how long (two hours), the expected work output (detailed notes), and how often (weekly). It also adds in a touch of accountability by promising to deliver these notes to your team once a week. That's a great goal!

> **A goal can be clear and attainable, but it will still be a bad goal if you don't apply some measurement to it.**

ENSURING GOAL ALIGNMENT

One last tip/warning in the area of goals: don't go crazy. People often start dreaming big and setting all sorts of goals once they get a sense of how powerful they can be. I'm all for having big goals in life and business, but your goals should always be taking you closer to your ultimate win. As you and your wife focus on your goals, make sure those goals align with:

- *Your pace*: Watch out for goals that look good on paper but require more time and effort than you and your wife want to put into the business.
- *Your contribution*: Make sure your goals line up with the two key contributions you identified in Chapter 8.
- *The compensation plan*: Don't allow for sideways energy that isn't producing income and moving your wife to the next rank. Stay focused!

Remember, you and your wife are a team, so you have a stake in the goals she's setting for the business. This isn't just *her thing*; it's your thing, too, so work *together* on your new team goals.

ACTION STEP

Walk your wife through this chapter in the next twenty-four hours. Ask her to identify a few CAM goals over the next day or two and set a time within the next three days to review those goals together. Once you agree on them together, post those goals where you'll both see them often. That will be your brand-new business scoreboard!

CHAPTER 10

CORNER MAN

As BECKIE BUILT HER BUSINESS, SHE AND I BECAME AWARE OF HOW many people were watching what she was doing and how she was doing it. Friends, family members, people at church, and even other women in her company talked to her about her methods and goals. I'd like to say all these people were curious because they were impressed and simply wanted to cheer her on and support her. Sadly, that wasn't the case. The harsh reality is that many of these people responded to her success in painfully negative ways. These critics gossiped about her, made up stories about her (or at least spread someone else's false stories), questioned her character, and made baseless assumptions and accusations about her recruitment tactics. Someone even spread a story about how she used our church directory to target people and pressure them into joining her team. Our church doesn't even have a directory!

So much of what we were hearing was absolutely crazy. It would have been funny—if it didn't hurt so much. These experiences took Beckie by surprise. Even after years as an entrepreneur, she was still caught off guard by how others often respond to someone else's success. It was devastating to her personally and damaged her confidence in her business. We learned the hard way that network marketing brings out the best in some people and the worst in others. Speaking as her husband, I found all the gossip, comparisons, competition, and jealousy just . . . *gross.* How can grown men and women act this way? How do they think this is an acceptable outlet for their own insecurities and lack of confidence? All this led to some painful experiences on Beckie's journey.

Not all the negative voices came from others, though; we also found this business brought some of Beckie's own internal struggles to the surface. She struggled with her confidence and competence. She faced uncertainty, hurt, isolation, and fear. She worried about what other women thought of her and why her character had been questioned. She wondered if she had what it took to push through the pain and achieve our big win. She second-guessed whether she really was taking advantage of her existing relationships in order to build a business. As we've worked with other network-marketing pros, we've found this is a pretty universal experience. Every woman in network marketing seems to face these questions—or attacks— along the way.

In many ways, network marketing is like a boxing match. Picture your wife in the ring fighting for your team goals and your big win. See her there fighting for financial independence for your family, a sense of purpose in her career, and the chance to help other families achieve their own dreams. What she's fighting for isn't easy, but it's worth it. So, like any good boxer, she stands her ground, punching and blocking and trying to stay in the fight long enough to go the distance. It's the heavyweight fight of her life, and she's doing great. But she needs help. She needs her *corner man.*

YOUR NEW ROLE

There will be times when your wife's insecurity is high and she's taking a pounding from internal and external voices. In those moments, no matter what your two sweet spot contributions are in her business, it's your job to be her corner man. In boxing, that's the guy who stands at the corner of the ring, intensely watching every jab and waiting for the bell to mark the end of the round. As soon as he hears that bell, he jumps into action. He puts a stool in the ring for his boxer. He squirts water in his mouth and checks his cuts and bruises. He makes sure the fighter still has his head on straight and is able to continue the fight. He gives encouragement, support, and advice to lead the fighter into the next round. The corner man has one minute every round to make sure his boxer has everything he needs to keep fighting. That is one of your most important roles in your wife's business—to help her keep fighting.

As her corner man, you have some key responsibilities *during* the fight, and we'll get to those in a minute. But first, I want you to understand your responsibilities before the fight ever starts. A boxer doesn't step into the ring unprepared; he has months of training—mental and physical—for the fight ahead. I realize that jumping into a boxing ring to get physically pummeled by another man isn't quite **It's your job to be her corner man.** the same as your wife preparing to teach a class, host a party, or have a phone call with a potential business builder. Sometimes, though, those things can seem just as intimidating. Her fight hasn't even started, but she already needs support. You can help her get ready.

Every corner man does three important things for his boxer before a fight: he limits distractions, gives him space to warm up, and speaks confidence to him. Those are three things we can do, too, to support our network-marketing wives. Maybe you could take care of the kids a little more, make sure the house is quiet during her work time, or step up with the housework.

How can you give her space to warm up? Everyone has a different definition of *space*, so ask her what she needs. If she's more introverted, she might need a day to herself to do some work and collect her strength. If she's more outgoing, she might prefer to go out with friends to clear her head before a big business event. Let her guide you, but be ready to follow through with what she needs.

How are you speaking confidence to her? I've found that it doesn't take much for me to make a huge impact on my wife's confidence. A simple "I believe in you," "You're doing great," or even "You got this" can go a long way. She probably doesn't need a long explanation from you on *why* you believe in her; she may just need to see that you really do believe she can do this. Sending her into a fight with a big vote of confidence is one of the most important things a corner man can do!

SUPPORT HER DURING THE FIGHT

No matter how good a job you do preparing her for the fight, things change a bit once she climbs into the ring. She'll win some rounds—hopefully *most* rounds—but she won't win every one. There are going to be some losses, and those losses are going to hurt. When she wins a round, such as signing a new business builder or hosting a successful party, you should come around her, celebrate her victory, help her catch her breath, and work to keep her momentum going. When she loses a round and comes back to her corner feeling defeated, it's your job to spring into action and lift her back up. That's when the corner man's role is essential. In that one minute you get to spend with her between rounds, you need to focus on three things: recovery, tactical advice, and motivation. Let's break those down a bit.

Recovery
In boxing, a corner man helps the fighter catch his breath and deals with any cuts and bleeding. As the corner man of your wife's business, how can you apply this to your ongoing support of her? Start with her breathing. No, she probably hasn't literally had the wind knocked out of her, but she might have lost sight of her reasons for doing this business in the first place. We talked about the importance

of her *win* earlier in this book. The *win* is like oxygen in her business. When that's knocked out of her, she'll start to fall apart. When you see that happen, you can come alongside her and remind her of all the reasons she chose this business and your ultimate win. That can breathe life back into her when setbacks have punched her in the gut. Also, if she's taken a few hits from naysayers and gossips, she may have some cuts and bruises to deal with. You can't take the sting out of her wounds, but you can be there to make sure they aren't fatal. You can do that by listening intently and gently offering your reassurance that she's doing a great job and you appreciate her sacrifice for your family.

Tactical Advice

A corner man often gives on-the-spot coaching and tactical advice in between boxing rounds. If you're like me, you can probably *always* come up with some well-meaning tips that can "turn things around." But we've got to be careful here. If you say too much, she could think you're trying to *fix* her or implying that she's not doing a good enough job. If you don't say enough, she might think

> **The *win* is like oxygen in her business.**

that you just don't care about her business at all. There's a fine line between interfering and ignoring, and you're probably going to fall on the wrong side of the line every now and then. That's okay. Try to get in the habit of holding your tongue until you know for sure what she needs. The best way I've found to figure this out is to simply ask, "What can I do to help?"

Motivation

A few rough rounds will take the fight out of the best champion. Your wife is no different. Every time she gets back in the ring after a defeat, she'll feel a little more insecure and unsure of herself. That's when you, her corner man, have to motivate and encourage her.

Help her process what she learned in her losses and apply that to her future efforts and go out of your way to ensure she doesn't waste any time beating herself up for any mistakes she may have made. Help her see the hope of future success rather than the sting of past failures. It's natural for her to feel a little timid as she leaves the corner and gets back in the fight, but she should hear you encouraging her from the corner as she steps back into the ring for the next round.

SKIP THE TONGUE-LASHINGS

Whether your wife is winning or losing in her business right now, you have an important role to play as her corner man. It's a responsibility to take seriously, but that doesn't mean you always need to be on her with an endless string of tips and tricks. And it definitely doesn't mean you should join her in a pity party when things are particularly tough. Instead, I choose to follow this advice from a real-life boxing corner man:

> In the immediate aftermath, I like to allow a boxer to bask in the glory of a win or savour the unpalatable truth of a defeat without interfering too much in either. Experiencing these feelings is a natural part of the process of fighting, and sport in general for that matter. The last thing that a boxer needs in the minutes following a fight is a tongue-lashing from a corner man.[5]

The post-fight tongue-lashing *won't* help her business and *will* hurt your relationship. Even if you think you have a crucial piece of advice after a big win or crippling loss, save it for another time. The emotional high or low immediately after a fight is not the time for you to try to solve all her problems.

---

5   "The Corner Man," MyBoxingCoach.com, November 3, 2011, https://www. myboxingcoach.com/the-corner-man/.

SECTION 2 WRAP-UP

Alright, that's another section in the books. Before we move on to this chapter's action step, let's quickly review the high points from this section. First, we saw that your wife's business isn't a solo sport; it isn't just *her* thing, it's *your family's* thing. That means approaching the business as a team. Second, I encouraged you to dig into the details of the compensation plan and get a better understanding of how your wife will win in her business. Third, I showed you how to identify your two key contributions that you can offer your wife's business. That's your sweet spot. Fourth, we saw this business (like any enterprise) needs strong team goals that are clear, attainable, and measurable. Finally, in this chapter, I showed you how you can serve your wife by embracing your role as her corner man.

Now that you are excited about the potential of your wife's business and have clarity about the role you can play, it's time to move on to Section 3: It's Game Time. There, we will see how all this plays out in real life as she builds her business.

ACTION STEP

The action step for this chapter is incredibly easy to complete, but it will be far more challenging to live out. Your job for this chapter is to commit to being your wife's corner man. Commit to help her prepare well for significant moments in her business. Commit to step in when she's a little beat up from a difficult meeting, handling a conflict, or suffering a setback in building her business. Commit to encourage and motivate her as she steps back into the ring!

Nate and Dana Moore
doTerra, Presidential Diamonds

My wife came home from teaching her first essential oils class at about 10:00 p.m. one night. From the moment she walked through the door, I could see an energy and a glow on her face that I hadn't seen in a long time. She was excited—*really excited*—about building a business, and I knew immediately that I had to support her. Finding my place in her business didn't happen overnight, but, over time, we figured out where I fit. Because I was more detailed-oriented and enjoyed playing around with numbers, we agreed that I could help with maximizing the compensation plan, team-member placement strategy, and dealing with the financials.

Within a year, her business was so successful that I was able to leave my six-figure office job and work alongside my wife full time in her business. What a change! The family had always depended on my income, but now I was able to be at home, work with my wife, and spend precious time with my four young children. In an age when so many people sacrifice family for money, my wife's business gave us the chance to head in the opposite direction. Now, thanks to my wife's amazing skills, a great team, an excellent business opportunity, and my help, we get to enjoy tons of family time while still making money together!

Transitioning from a full-time job to being at home helping my wife grow her business wasn't always easy, and we definitely had a few bumps in the road. Over time, though, we learned what worked best for both of us. That's when the real fun began. We found out that if you have two people who are focused on the same goal and working together to achieve it, you can be exponentially more successful *and* improve your marriage along the way!

SECTION 3

IT'S GAME TIME

CHAPTER 11

KNOW YOUR SEASON

WHEN BECKIE FIRST STARTED BUILDING HER BUSINESS, I KIND OF assumed every month would be the same. I figured each month she'd talk to the same number of people, add the same number of business builders, and have the same amount of sales. I knew her numbers would likely increase each month as she grew her business, but I thought it would be steady, month-to-month growth. I assumed we'd have some stability and consistency in the time she spent on the business and income it brought in. I was wrong on pretty much every count!

I missed the obvious fact that network marketing, like any business, has unique rhythms and seasons. For example, the end of the month is huge for Beckie. In the last two or three days of the month, she and her whole team are scrambling to get last-minute orders, hit their ranks, and meet their income goals. They're also doing a lot of admin work as they try to organize their volume to make the most of the compensation plan and slot their new business builders in the best place within their organizations. And then there's the last-minute phone calls, meetings, and strategy sessions to squeeze every last bit of opportunity out of the month. Beckie probably gets a hundred text messages and phone calls in the last day or two from people who need advice or encouragement. It's a mad dash to midnight on the last day of the month. Then, when the month is finally closed and everyone's taken care of, Beckie usually falls into bed exhausted around 1:00 a.m.

The next morning—the first day of the month—she generally stays in bed a little late and grumbles when she finally makes an appearance. I can always tell how tired she is. She's proud of her work and her team, of course, but still tired. It's not uncommon for her to give herself the day off to make the mental and emotional transition from the hectic end of one month to the new beginning of the next. And then the cycle starts all over again.

As clueless as I was in the beginning, I learned pretty quickly that there are rhythms and seasons to my wife's business. Each month goes mostly as I described, but the intensity goes up and down depending on what time of year it is. In Beckie's business, the company focuses a lot of energy and discounts around three big months a year. For one week in each of those months, they offer incredible sales and discounts that result in huge sales volume for her and her team. She works her tail off during those weeks, but the payoff is worth it. Then, summer is generally a slow period. It's more difficult to get people to attend classes and workshops during the summer, so everything slows down and it's hard to build momentum. Finally, the company has a huge national convention in September and kicks off their new season of high activity. That's the natural rhythm of Beckie's business, and it's a schedule we've had to get used to. Your wife's business may have different high and low periods, but I'm sure it has some kind of seasonal swings. If you want to really understand the business and support your wife when she needs it the most, you've got to figure out what the seasons look like for her business.

Network marketing, like any business, has unique rhythms and seasons.

NAVIGATING THE SEASONS

For a basketball fan, nothing compares to March Madness. There's just something thrilling about a single-elimination tournament full of Cinderella stories, upsets, and powerhouse schools going head to head, all vying for the top spot on the final bracket. Even though the NCAA tournament is the pinnacle of the college basketball season, it's not the *only* part of the teams' year. Most people may only pay attention to them in March, but these players and coaches work year-round, spending the *other* eleven months preparing for the big tournament. They spend hundreds of hours practicing, conditioning, and watching game film during the off-season. This prepares them for tournaments at the beginning of the season to see where they stand and where they need to improve. Then they move into some non-conference games to get them ready for the grind of conference play. Next, they finish their conference tournament, where they're hopefully firing on all cylinders and punch their card to the Big Dance.

Knowing what season they are in at any given time keeps teams focused on what's important at the moment.

Knowing what season they are in at any given time keeps teams focused on what's important *at the moment*. They aren't worried about winning games in the off-season, for example; that's not what the off-season is for. In the same way, understanding the different seasons of your wife's business will help you get a handle on what she's doing (and what you need to be doing) throughout the year. Over the past few years, Beckie and I have identified four steps for navigating the seasons and trends of her business. Even though the seasons may be unique to her particular company, these principles can apply to any network-marketing business.

Know the Rhythm of Her Seasons

This first step is a no-brainer, but you need to write down the seasonal rhythm of your wife's business. In Beckie's business, for example, I've identified the four specific seasons I mentioned earlier. They are:

1. The last two days of each month
2. The three big months (with special discounts and incentives)
3. The summer slowdown
4. The national convention / new-season kickoff

If your wife's been active in the business for a while, you probably already know enough detail to sketch out an annual overview of what her year looks like, which months are particularly busy, when her off-season typically is, and so on. Even if you know it intuitively, I suggest writing it down. Putting it on paper makes it more *real* and helps you keep it in front of you when you need a refresher. If you aren't able to map out the flow of her business by memory, ask her to walk you through it. You can't support her and maximize opportunities if you don't understand how the seasons work.

Know the Expectations for Each Season

Each season has different demands on your wife—and on you. She'll need different kinds of help from you depending on what season she's in and what's going on in the business at any given time. When you know the seasons, you will probably *intuitively* know how to best support her work. But let's take that a step further by writing down some specific ways to help your wife through each of the different seasons. Here's what that looks like for me as I try to support Beckie's efforts:

1. **The last two days of each month:** She's going to be extremely busy and won't have much time for anything outside of the business. I need to be available to cover whatever the kids need on those days, and I'm going to take responsibility for

dinners and any random tasks that pop up so she can focus on closing out the month without distraction.

2. **The three big months (with special discounts and incentives):** Since we know these will be busy months, we'll have a special calendaring session at the start of the month to make sure I'm available to cover the kids' appointments, sports practices, and games as needed. I'll also help her create sales goals and act as a sounding board as she works out her business strategy for those months of high activity.

3. **The summer slowdown:** We expect everything to slow down during the summer, so I go into it knowing her income and momentum will temporarily drop. I also don't expect her to advance in rank much (if at all) during the summer. The good news is this will be a season of rest for our family, and we'll find fun things to do together while life isn't as hectic.

4. **The national convention / new season kickoff:** This is basically New Year's Day for her business, so I'll give her space to focus on motivating her team and gear up for the new season. I also know she'll probably be out of town for a few days to attend the convention, so I can plan my work and social schedule accordingly.

Now it's your turn. Go through the seasonal overview you wrote down and add a line or two to each phase indicating how you will support her in that specific season.

Choose Intentional Imbalance

Everyone seems to be talking about *work–life balance* these days. It's like people are trying to figure out the magic formula for creating total harmony and consistency in their schedules. Guess what: it's never going to happen. In my opinion, there's no such thing as a work–life balance that's going to hold true every day, every week, every month, and every year. Each season is different. Some months, your work will simply demand more time from you. Other times, your family will demand more. When you're sick, your health will demand more. When your church is focused on a big initiative, church will demand more. During your kids' sports seasons, that commitment will demand more. Why are we driving ourselves crazy, then, trying to find some mythical balance?

Instead, I recommend striving for what I call *intentional imbalance*. Look at each season and identify where your time and energy will be best spent *for that season*. And know that you won't be able to do everything; thinking you can will only set you—and your family—up for failure. For our family, rather than trying to figure out ways to do *more*, we've started figuring out ways to do *less*. We focus on each season, set our priorities for that specific season, and then give ourselves permission to forget about everything else for a while. We even started writing a Stop-Doing List as an antidote to the never-ending to-do lists many of us seem to live by.

You'll never be able to give everything in your life equal time, energy, and attention. So try something different and embrace intentional imbalance instead.

Make Time for R&R (Rest and Reward)

The NBA and MLB have All-Star breaks, and the NFL gets bye weeks. Why? Playing the game is what these guys do for a living, so why do they have time off built into their schedules? It's for the same reason you have vacation time and off days built into your job. If you work and work and work every day, nonstop, with no rest, you'll burn out (or go crazy). We aren't machines; we need regular rest. In network marketing, though, it can be hard to see the line between work and personal life. After all, network-marketing pros work nights and weekends, often with their friends and family. And, in most cases, the work is fun! We can't forget that it's still work, though. For that reason, you and your wife need to be intentional about building R&R—rest and reward—into her business. She needs time when she knows she *won't* work, time that's 100 percent dedicated to rest and relaxation.

This is also where you could throw in some rewards for all her hard work. They don't have to be expensive, but they should be intentional and meaningful. Get her a small gift, take her to dinner (without the kids), surprise her with a spa day, or make arrangements for her to have a day out with her girlfriends. These little surprises breathe life into her, and they can breathe new life into her business, as well.

RESPECT THE SEASONS

Let me be blunt as we wrap up this chapter. If you fail to understand and respect the seasons of your wife's business, you will set yourself up for constant conflict, frustration, and disappointment. Even a sweet, loving gesture can go painfully wrong if you don't pay attention to her busy seasons. For example, trying to whisk Beckie away for a weekend getaway at the end of the month would blow up in my face! Not only would it put pressure on her to ignore her business when it needs her the most, but it would show her that I'm not paying attention. That same gift at the right time, though, would mean the world to her. When you show your wife how much you love her by learning the rhythms of her business, you'll help turn every season into a *winning* season.

ACTION STEP

Throughout this chapter, I already gave you some work to do, so your action step is to actually *do it*. Walk back through the four steps for navigating the seasons in this chapter. Write down the seasons of her business and how you will support her during each one. Then, identify how each season should be intentionally imbalanced by writing down what will need more attention and what you can set aside for that season. Finally, plan some rest and reward for your wife. Make sure it fits during her season of rest and encourage her to use the time to unplug. All this shows her that you're invested in her success and that you really are paying attention to her business!

CHAPTER 12

READY, SET, GO!

I'VE SAID SEVERAL TIMES THAT I'M A HUGE SPORTS FAN. FOOTBALL, basketball, baseball—you name it, I love it. As much as I enjoy and follow team sports, one thing that has always fascinated me is individual Olympic events. I'm talking about things like swimming, track and field, and skiing. The stakes are so incredibly high for these athletes. In the team sports we normally watch, the players work together and have weekly (sometimes daily) games to compete against one another. With many Olympic events, however, an athlete will train all alone for four years to participate in an event that may last less than one minute. I can't even imagine that kind of pressure when the day finally comes. Picture yourself training several years to compete in the 100-meter dash. When the day comes, you have to push down the nerves, fear, anxiety, and anticipation and force yourself on the starting blocks. You stand there, every muscle fiber locked and ready, waiting for the gun to go off. When you hear that sound, no matter how you feel or how ready you are, you have to run! Anyone who hesitates at the starting line or lingers a fraction of a second too long will lose.

In network marketing, your wife trains year-round by planning, learning comp plans, practicing presentations, learning what to say to potential business builders, and getting familiar with her product or service, but none of that training matters if she never gets off the starting blocks. She can train for years and years, but she'll never even *compete* in this business if she doesn't run when it's time to run.

THERE'S NO STARTING PISTOL

Olympians take off as soon as they hear the gun. Sadly, you and your wife won't hear a clear, definitive blast to let you know when it's time to get moving. It'd be nice, though, wouldn't it? Sometimes it'd be helpful to have an explosion that gets our attention and wakes us up from our isolated planning and practice and sends us off to work to make the contacts we need to make, talk to the people we need to talk to, teach the classes we need to teach, and so on. But we don't get a countdown. There's no 3–2–1 or ready–set–go coming. Nobody's going to knock on our door and tell us when it's time to get going; we have to do that for ourselves.

That's true in network marketing, and it's true in every other part of our lives. It's up to us to put our plans into motion. Heck, I've even seen this play out in how I've approached this book. I spent months *thinking* about writing this book, but I kept putting it off. Whenever I thought about calling someone to help me or talking to a publisher, I stalled. My feet were stuck in the starting blocks for months until I finally pried them lose and got to work.

It's often the start that stops people.

Legendary baseball Hall of Famer Reggie Jackson once said, "You can't steal second base *and* keep one foot on first." At some point, you have to step off the bag and go for it! A harsh reality of life is that it's often the start that stops people. Most of us never accomplish our goals because we go right up to the starting line, get in our starting positions, and then walk away. We often never do the thing we want to do because we're too scared, intimidated, overwhelmed, or downright lazy to actually start. That kind of failure to launch will wreck your life in a hundred different ways, but it will absolutely demolish any hope you and your wife have of building a successful network-marketing business. If you want to win, you've got to start.

GET OFF THE STARTING BLOCK

One of the best things about network marketing is the freedom it provides. It allows you and your wife to run your business from anywhere, work at your own pace, put in as many (or as few) hours as you want, and build as big as you want. However, I've seen many women (and their husbands) use that freedom as an excuse to put off doing the work that needs to be done. Then later, when things don't work out and they fail to build a successful business, they blame the business model. That's easier than facing the fact that they never got off their butts and actually did anything to build the business. They let their fear and intimidation—or, more likely, their lack of self-discipline—steal the potential from their business aspirations. To be blunt, they never left the starting blocks and then complained about not winning the race.

We can talk about goals, wins, and sweet spots all day long, but every ounce of planning and preparation will fall short if you and your wife never actually get to work. So how do you get in the race? How do you keep from getting stuck before you ever get started? Here are three tips for getting off the starting block.

Create a Sense of Urgency

We saw before that good goals require a deadline and specific time frame. That gives them *urgency*. If you make your goals and their deadlines non-negotiable, you attach an undeniable sense of urgency to them. You know when they're due, so you know you need to get started on them. None of us should be a stranger to deadlines, either. We had them in school, we have them at work, we have them in our health and fitness goals; deadlines are everywhere, so why would you leave them out of your network-marketing business?

Urgency is the secret sauce that drives our success. It increases focus, ramps up our motivation, gives us built-in accountability, amplifies a sense of teamwork when working with others, and enables us to achieve more than we thought we could do faster than we thought we could do it. Urgency is powerful stuff! However, like we've said, no one is going to magically appear and force deadlines into your wife's business; she has to do that for herself. And those deadlines are going to require sacrifice—not just from her but from you, as well. That's why it is so important for you both to get a vision for your big win early on. Deadlines and urgency force you to stick to your guns and keep working hard even when you don't want to. In those times of low motivation, you both must cling even more tightly to the *win* you identified earlier in this book. (You *have* done that by now, right?)

Do Something Every Day

Beckie always tells her team members, "Building your business is easy to do—and easy *not* to do." I love that advice. When you get right down to it, network marketing is a really easy way to build a business. It really comes down to two simple things: share a great product or service you believe in with other people and then find others to do the same thing with you. However, since it's your own business and no one is forcing you to "go into the office" every day, it can be easy to let days and weeks go by without doing anything. It's not like you have a boss waiting for you to punch a time clock every day!

In your wife's business, *she's* the boss. She's the one she's accountable to. She's the one waiting and watching for her to do something that moves her business forward. If she doesn't, no one will come chasing after her. It's up to her to commit to do something—at least *one thing*—that will move the business forward every single day. It doesn't have to be a huge thing, but it needs to be big enough to move her at least an inch closer to her goals.

One word of warning here: it's not your job to act like her boss. It's *her* business, remember? You can (and should) hold her accountable to the goals she's set, but you can't try to boss her around or make her feel guilty for not doing as much as you think she should in a day. Trust me; that conversation never goes well. You can, however, go back to your two key contributions from Chapter 8 and use them to create some simple daily actions. In fact, your daily *something* could simply be asking her what she did that day to advance her goals and then engaging with her as she answers.

Quit the Excuses

Think about one thing you've committed to do to help move your wife's business forward—something you *should* have started by now but haven't. You got something in mind? Now, ask yourself, *Why haven't I started this yet?*

"Building your business is easy to do—and easy not to do."

If you're like me, you'd probably say, "I've been too busy. X, Y, and Z popped up and stole the time I was going to commit to her business." Or maybe you'd say, "I was going to do it, but my wife needs me to do *this* instead." I've used both of these excuses before, and they were as lame for me then as they are for you now. These are deflections, a way to excuse my own negligence or laziness by blaming something else. The truth is, however, I was the problem; I was the reason those things didn't get done. And, if you haven't done something you told your wife you'd do, then *you're* the problem; *you're* the reason those things didn't get done. Welcome to the club.

So, let's try it again. Ask yourself, *Why haven't I started yet?* Keep pushing past the first few answers that pop into your head. Dig through all the excuses until the *real* answers come through—the answers you'd be embarrassed to tell someone else. We usually hide behind our excuses, but it's time to tear them down. Your wife knows you better than anyone on earth, and she isn't fooled by the excuses you've given her for not helping her. It's time to get down to the truth—even if that truth hurts.

MORE IS SAID THAN DONE

About a year into Beckie's business, we discussed ways I could contribute and decided that I could help by creating some video training for her team. Most of the women she worked with didn't have much experience leading and managing other people, but that was something I'd been doing for two decades. I've also done a ton of training over the years, so we knew this would be a way for me to make an impact in her business. I agreed to do it, we made some plans to film it, and then . . . I stalled.

> It's time to get down to the truth—even if that truth hurts.

Weeks went by, and I hadn't done anything toward this goal. Beckie asked me about it several times, and I always came up with a weak excuse. Life is always busy for us, so it was easy to find something to blame for my lack of follow-through. I just kept passing the buck and telling Beckie I'd do it later. But "later" never came.

Finally, I realized she was getting frustrated with me—and that I deserved it. I looked in the mirror and asked myself why I'd been putting this simple task off for so long. When I dug past all the obvious excuses, the truth hit me: I was scared. I was afraid that the women who watched the training would think I was a bad teacher or that I couldn't come up with anything useful that would help their businesses. I felt like I was putting my own reputation as a leader on the line, and that scared me off. Once I got passed that excuse, I was able to create some urgency with a self-imposed deadline and do the daily work required to hit my goal. And, as it turns out, I was able to put together some training that helped a lot of Beckie's team members. Beckie loved it, and I heard nothing but positive feedback from her team. Looking back, I'm embarrassed that I wasted so much time being scared about it.

When all is said and done, more is said than done. Don't be the guy who always *talks* about his contribution but never *does* anything. If you want to win the race, you've got to run!

ACTION STEP

The action step for this chapter is to get off the starting block. Identify one thing you should have started but haven't, ask yourself why you're stalled (the real reason), and get started on it today. Then, ask your wife to review this chapter and do the same thing. Finally, sit down with her and discuss how you can encourage each other to create urgency, do something for the business every day, and quit excusing your inaction.

CHAPTER 13

THRIVE IN THE GRIND

AT **THE START OF THIS SECTION,** I **SHARED THE SEASONS AND** rhythms of Beckie's business and suggested you figure out the same for your wife's business. It's crucial to know when the highs and lows are going to hit. Like I said earlier, Beckie's main high times are the three months a year when her company offers huge discounts on their products. Those specials create sales and volume more than any other time of the year. Beckie and her team stay crazy busy for most of that month, and almost everyone seems to advance in rank during those sales. All that success and activity create momentum for Beckie and her business builders that energizes their businesses for months afterward. They work a lot during those weeks, but they also see an almost immediate reward for their efforts. Beckie's learned how to focus her team around their goals during the high tide and strategically leverage those critical months for continued success throughout the year. Those months are full of hard work and sacrifice, but they are so worth it.

Now, let's look at the flip side of the coin. What about the normal months of the year when business seems harder, when it's much more difficult to make sales and add new builders to your team? There are fewer rank advancements, no big income spikes, and it feels like there is very little new momentum at all. These are the months I call "the grind"—the seasons when it takes incredible discipline and willpower to keep working the business. It can be so easy for less-motivated business builders to take days, weeks, and even entire months off from the business during these times. When there isn't a clear connection between effort and reward, it can be hard to force yourself to make your calls, set up parties, and develop your skills. So, when the business slows down, the business owner is tempted to slow down, as well.

DON'T FALL FOR TRAP GAMES

Believe it or not, this season—*the grind*—is when network-marketing champions rise or fall. Some builders use the slower weeks to focus, plan, prepare, and bear down harder on their goals; other builders allow the less-demanding season to distract them, cause them to lose focus, and give them an excuse for falling into lazy, unproductive habits. They convince themselves that the slower periods aren't important to their businesses, so they take their eyes off the ball.

The grind is when network-marketing champions rise or fall.

I see this happen all the time in sports. Has your favorite team ever suffered a surprising loss to a weaker team the week before a highly anticipated matchup? These are called "trap games"—what should be an easy win the week before a big game turns into an embarrassing defeat. Why? Because the team was more focused on the big game in the future than the easy game right under their noses. They don't take the weaker opponent seriously because they're so focused on the rival showdown that's still a week out. Everyone's always shocked when this happens, but it makes perfect sense. It's exhilarating to go all-in preparing to dominate a rival, but it's not easy for a team to work hard, practice, run drills, and sacrifice for a game they barely see as a blip on the radar. The team falls apart in the grind because they don't take it seriously.

The same thing happens to thousands of network-marketing business builders every day. The average network-marketing business is more about thriving in the grind of a normal month—when everything is slower, the tasks feel monotonous, and the whole thing feels boring and uneventful—than it is about riding the wave of the high months.

STAYING FOCUSED IN THE GRIND

It doesn't take much effort to get pumped up for a big event, but what about the small events? What about the non-events? How do you get (and stay) excited for those? How can you encourage your wife to stay focused and thrive in the grind? I can think of four ways. Let's run through them and see how you can apply them to your wife's business.

Remember Your **Win** and Focus on Your Goals

One of the first things you and your wife should have done when she started her business is clearly define *why* she's doing the business and identify what winning looks like for her and your family. I've hammered that pretty hard throughout the book so far, and this is one of the main reasons: if you don't know your *win* and you can't remember your goals for the business, you and your wife will fall apart during the grind seasons. When you can't see an immediate result from her hard work, you have to keep your eyes on the long-term win.

The grind may not be exciting, but it's a crucial step toward getting where you want to go. This whole business is a journey, and each step is important. If you stop walking when the path gets dull and boring, you'll never reach the mountaintop you've been dreaming of. Something that might be helpful in the grind is for you and your wife to create a dream board. This can be a simple sign or poster you and your wife make with pictures of her big goals. If she wants to earn enough money to take the family on a trip to Hawaii, then the two of you can fill the board up with pictures of Hawaii. If she's saving up for a new car, then you can fill the board with pictures of her dream car. Whatever goal she's set for her business, pin it to the board and keep it where you both can see it—especially during the slow months when it can be hard to maintain focus.

Keep Doing the Little Things

How do you climb a mountain? One step at a time. How do you eat an elephant? One bite at a time. How do you build a successful network-marketing business? One sale/call/contact at a time. Yes, she'll have bursts of activity during the busy seasons when everything seems to click and every investment she makes into the business comes back to her tenfold. A lot of people think those are the times that make or break their network-marketing success; they think they can build a business around just a few key moments a year. But nope! It doesn't work that way! That's like thinking you can build a superhero body by working out four or five times a year. No matter how intense those workouts are, they won't deliver the results you want. Instead, you have to show up and do the work *every day*—whether you want to or not, whether anyone sees you or not, and whether the gym is crowded or not. It's the small daily decisions that, over time, can turn a weak, flabby body (and business) into a strong, fit powerhouse.

The grind may not be exciting, but it's a crucial step toward getting where you want to go.

If you and your wife want to be successful in this business, you've got to do the little things—the *boring* things—better than anyone else. This includes things like following up on customers over and over again, prioritizing time for training and personal development, carving out time to learn everything there is to know about the products, learning from other successful people, keeping the steady drumbeat of social media going, and inviting new people to join every week. The little things aren't really *fun*; I get that. But the impact of doing them consistently over time will *make* it fun when you and your wife hit your goals and achieve your ultimate win.

Maximize Your Return on Luck

I'm not a big believer in luck *per se*, but I've been around long enough to know there are some opportunities that just seem to fall in your lap. In network marketing, that could look like a new customer who falls in love with the product and wants to tell everyone they've ever met about it. Or, it could be a random social media post you put up on a whim that ended up getting thousands of views and shares. Or, someone may offer to throw a product party for you at their home and twenty people show up out of nowhere. I love it when this stuff happens!

I've seen every one of those "lucky" things happen in Beckie's business multiple times. As great as they are, these events in isolation didn't make a big dent in her business. It's usually not the opportunity itself that moved the needle; it's how she *maximized* the opportunity that makes all the difference. Jim Collins talks about this in his book *Great by Choice*.[6] There, he explains that the big surprise is great, but the real magic happens when you go about the tedious work of squeezing every drop of opportunity out of it. That almost always requires a bunch of extra work you weren't expecting and probably weren't prepared for. I can promise you from experience, though: if you and your wife *don't* maximize the opportunity, you will never know how much further that random, *lucky* event could have taken you toward your goals.

6   Jim Collins, *Great by Choice* (New York: HarperBusiness, 2011).

Celebrate the Small Things

If you only celebrate the mountaintop moments, that is all you'll ever see as success, and you'll miss the daily, mundane wins that truly build a strong business. They'll be so small they'll just sneak past you. But, if you build a consistent rhythm of celebrating the small things your wife does to build her business, you'll set yourself up to see wins every single day. That's how you thrive in the grind, by opening your eyes to the small wins that trickle in here and there no matter what season you're in.

If you want to see more big wins, you've got to learn how to celebrate the small ones. Celebrate if your wife follows up with three existing customers and gets a new order from one of them. Celebrate that she met her personal-development goal of reading a business or leadership book for fifteen minutes a day, five days straight. Celebrate that she talked to four new people about her business opportunity this week, even if none of them joined her team. Celebrate that you're both working together on this and using her business as an opportunity to dream together about the kind of life you want for your family. These are all awesome things! These things are making you better people and building a stronger marriage, so celebrate!

If you want to see more big wins, you've got to learn how to celebrate the small ones.

ATTENTION VS. ATTRITION

Network marketing is a business of attrition; if you don't pay attention to it every single day, your business will start to shrink. The daily tasks in the grind may not seem like much—they may not seem important at all—but they will make or break any network-marketing business. I once heard a coach say, "The level of your *game* is determined by the level of your *grind*." Nowhere is that truer than in network marketing. If you and your wife are committed to seeing this business through every day, in both busy and slow seasons, you can build something you'll both be proud of. Yes, you need to keep an eye on the mountaintop, but don't forget to keep the other eye on the path in front of you. You won't be able to climb up the mountain if you can't even walk the simple, flat path ahead. Don't stumble when it's simple; make every step count for your business.

> **"The level of your game is determined by the level of your grind."**

ACTION STEP

The action step for this chapter is easy: write down one task you and your wife don't like to do and have minimized for a while because it doesn't seem important or big enough. Think about the impact it would have on the business, over time, if you both took that task more seriously during the grind. Commit to focus on that little chore every day for the next month and see how it pays off for you.

CHAPTER 14

LEVEL UP

HANNAH WAS ONE OF THE FIRST BUSINESS BUILDERS TO JOIN MY wife's team. She is a powerhouse in many aspects of her business. In fact, even after all this time, she's one of the best at promoting the product, getting new customers, and giving world-class customer service. She believes in the product and genuinely loves serving other people. Everyone loves Hannah, and she consistently has high personal sales volume every month. Sounds like a network-marketing champ, right? Well ... almost.

There's one enormous problem in Hannah's business, and it's one she simply will not address. She hasn't recruited another business builder to join her team in more than two years. As open and excited as she is about talking about the product, she simply can't bring herself to talk about the business opportunity side of things. When it comes to having those conversations, this bright, friendly sales pro freezes up. She goes out of her way to avoid recruiting other people to join her. Beckie has had several conversations with Hannah about this, and most of them end in tears. Beckie has told her a dozen times that she'll never be able to *level up* in this business by advancing in rank if she doesn't develop this skill. And every time, Hannah says she wants to do it, she wants to grow her business, and she wants to achieve her goals. So, she commits to talking to people about the opportunity and doing her best to add new team members ... but she never follows through. Hannah is stuck.

Her husband, Brent, is a great guy and super supportive of her. However, Brent won't step up and challenge Hannah to address her fears. Instead, he simply tells her, "I get it. I wouldn't want to do that either." He's letting her off the hook and actively encourages her to ignore the part of the business that makes her uncomfortable. This is so frustrating to watch! Hannah could literally double her income—I'm talking thousands more per month—if she could just find two people to build a business with. But she won't do it, and her husband won't challenge her to do it. If something doesn't change, she will never reach her full potential in this business because she's flat-out refusing to do the intimidating work required to level up.

After watching Hannah and dozens of other women go through this or similar struggles, I can make a prediction about your wife's business: there will come a time when she gets stuck. At some point, she will realize there is something significant she must overcome in order to level up and hit her goals. Like Hannah, it may be something she doesn't *want* to do. It might scare or intimidate her. She may not think she has the skill set to do it. It might require a level of vulnerability she's not ready to show. Whatever the reason, the day is coming when she will get stuck and feel like there's no way to move forward. And, if she stays there for too long, she will quit the business in frustration. If you truly want to support your wife in her network-marketing work, you've got to bear some of the responsibility here. When she gets stuck, it's your job to give her the encouragement she needs to get moving again.

ROOT VS. FRUIT

The really frustrating thing about Hannah is that she's great at the sales side of the business. She's built up a surprisingly strong income focusing on sales alone. As wonderful as that is and as much of a blessing as it's been for her family, she's missing out on the key piece of the network-marketing puzzle. Adding builders to her team creates exponential growth. I can hardly imagine how much she could earn every month if she built a team of other women and trained them all how to sell as well as she does. That thought blows my mind! But she won't do it. She's just focused on sales and is trying to convince herself that she can hit her goals while ignoring half the business model. Hannah and her husband are tripping over the belief that what she's been successful at so far—sales

Discover the root issue, not the fruit issue.

alone—will keep her business going long-term. But it won't. Hannah's starting to realize that what got her to *this point* will not take her to the *next level*. At every level in any business, you need to continually add new skills to your tool kit. What brought you success in the first year probably won't bring you continued success in year five and beyond. The old business adage is true: you're either moving forward or you're moving backward; there's no such thing as standing still.

But what should we reasonably expect Brent to do in this situation? What would *you* do? How much responsibility do we, as husbands, have when we see our wives stuck in their businesses? What should we do when we see them give in to fear and insecurity? How much should we encourage them to keep pressing on, and when should we keep our mouths shut? I'm not going to lie; this is like tiptoeing through a minefield. Any little misstep could blow up in our faces. That said, I have figured out a key principle that should help you navigate around the biggest land mines in this critical time in your wife's business. You should highlight this statement and maybe even write it down somewhere you'll see often. Here it is: Discover the *root issue*, not the *fruit issue*. I'll say it again for emphasis: Discover the *root issue*, not the *fruit issue*. But what does that mean?

As a pastor, I have spent thousands of hours counseling people about everything from addiction to parenting, marriage, emotional struggles, depression, and finances—you name it, I've counseled on it. At some point in every conversation, as the person shares their struggle, my mind moves to the root-vs.-fruit principle. You see, people usually start off by telling me their *fruit issues*. These are the outward issues you can see, just like fruit on a tree. They'll say something like, "I always blow up in anger," "I keep spending money," or, "I had an affair." But I don't care about the fruit issues; those are seldom the *real* problem that needs to be addressed. The true issues are always the *root issues*, the things just below the surface that no one can see. Even though they're hidden, these root issues are the foundation for everything else. This is where the angry outbursts, uncontrolled spending, and infidelity come from. I've learned that if I can dig past the fruit issue and find the root issue at the heart of the problem, we can do some real work. And, once the root issue is dealt with, the fruit issues will take care of themselves.

The true issues are always the root issues, the things just below the surface that no one can see.

It's often excruciatingly difficult for someone to admit his root issues to himself, let alone to a spouse or counselor. However, they're usually very easy to discover if you know where and how to look. In fact, in all my years of working with people, I've found that most root issues come down to four main things: fear, selfishness, insecurity, and people-pleasing. Probably 90 percent of all the fruit issues I've seen throughout my career can be traced back to one of those four things.

These root issues, however, have enormous power in our lives. When we give into fear, selfishness, insecurity, and people-pleasing, we allow ourselves to be held back from big things we want to accomplish. They cause pain in our lives because we surrender our goals and dreams to them. If you look back to Hannah's story at the start of this chapter, you can quickly see that her fruit issue—not wanting to talk about the network-marketing business opportunity—grew out of one of these four root issues. Maybe the fear of rejection or deep-seated insecurity kept her from telling people about the business. Or maybe it was a desire to please other people that prevented her from bringing it up. Whatever her specific root issue is, she'll never level up in this business until she uproots it and deals with it for good. I hope she does someday soon—and I hope her husband helps.

NAVIGATING THE J-CURVE

Getting past our root issues and moving into uncomfortable actions isn't easy. In fact, things will likely get worse—*more uncomfortable*—before they get better. This reminds me of the simple J curve you often see in economics. Basically, the J-curve pattern refers to a sharp decline at the beginning that then turns into steep growth.

Let's apply this to network marketing.

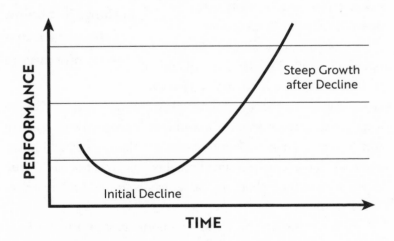

If your wife, like Hannah, refuses to recruit builders due to a root issue of fear, pushing past that root issue will likely lead to even more fear at first as she begins to talk to people about the opportunity. That's the initial dip in the J curve. Then, as she gets more comfortable and begins to see some positive results by adding new builders, things will start to turn around. Her confidence, business, number of builders, and income will all start to skyrocket because she pushed past that initial drop.

You could apply the root-vs.-fruit principle and J-curve model to practically any other issue. Here's another example:

- **Fruit Issue:** Low sales volume.
- **Root Issue:** Insecurity about suggesting her product as a solution for someone else's problem.
- **J-curve Dip:** Forcing herself to tell people about her product will cause an initial rush of fear and increased insecurity.
- **J-curve Increase:** Confidence rises as the product helps people, sales increase, and she gets more comfortable selling.

The challenge of the J curve is that people will be tempted to quit after the initial dip before things get better. But, if you and your wife can push through the pain (and there *will* be pain), you both can come out on the other side having beaten something that's likely been a limiting factor for most of your lives. When that happens, you will experience a new sense of power and freedom that's impossible to put into words!

> **Be the husband who acknowledges her root issue without judgment or condemnation and then challenges her to overcome it.**

HELP HER PUSH PAST THE PAIN

That's what I want you to do for your wife. I want you to be the husband who acknowledges her root issue without judgment or condemnation and then challenges her to overcome it. You can't do this by forcing her to do something she isn't ready to do or jump into something that genuinely terrifies her. But you *can* do it by giving her a safe space to examine her fear, selfishness, insecurity, or need to please other people. Get the root issue out of the dirt, clean it off, shine a light on it, and start to talk about it. Help her picture what her business—and her whole life—could look like if she finally got past an issue that's always held her back.

Then, once she's ready to address the root issue, commit with her to do the hard work required to level up. Root issues are powerful barriers in our lives, and it takes an even more powerful commitment to push past them. She will need your encouragement and support to make this significant change in her life. But when she does, you'll both share in an incredible victory, knowing you've achieved something together that neither of you could have done alone. That won't just level up her business; it will level up your marriage!

ACTION STEP

For this chapter's action step, I want you to carefully consider and answer the following questions:

1. Which root issue is most likely holding you back from leveling up in something you want to achieve for yourself?

2. Which root issue is most likely holding your wife back from leveling up in her business?

3. How can you start the conversation with your wife about this without making her feel judged or defensive? In your experience, would it be best to have her read this chapter, or should you bring it up some other way?

4. Where are you and your wife on the J curve in her business? If you're stuck in the dip, what would it take for you both to push through to the next level?

CHAPTER 15

PREPARE FOR THE NEXT SEASON

EVERY GOOD COACH AND PLAYER KNOWS THAT NO SEASON IS TRULY over until you've taken a good, hard look at where you've been and where you're heading. My high school soccer coach drilled that lesson into my head when I was a teenager. After each season, he met with the players one-on-one and in groups to go over the key takeaways from that year and how we needed to apply those lessons for the year ahead. One year, he met with me privately and shared his goals for the upcoming season. He was confident that we could have one of the best records in the league that year if we could focus on and master a few key things. He also told me I had a good shot at being a captain if I could improve in some specific areas and bring my overall level of fitness up. That was exactly the kind of motivation I needed. I worked my tail off during the off-season, came back stronger and more determined than ever, and earned the team captain position. Our coach inspired the whole team to give everything we had, and we brought home the state championship that year.

Looking back more than twenty years later, I can remember every detail of the conversation with the coach, the training I did, the hard practices we endured, and the thrill of winning the state title. My coach taught me a valuable lesson. He showed me that preparing for what's next must be a priority, because preparation paves the way for success. He had an honest evaluation of what we'd accomplished in the season that was ending, so he knew what we were capable of the next season. Then, my coach prepared a customized plan to get us where we wanted to go and cast a vision for what we could accomplish if we did the hard work of following through. He showed us in a meaningful way that preparation is powerful.

Too many network-marketing business owners focus all their time and energy on the season at hand. They think, *If I can just get to the end of this month/year/sales push, I'll be okay and can rest.* They set goals in isolation and never see how one year's momentum flows into the next. They don't bother setting goals until the new season is already starting, and, by then, the wins and losses of the previous season are already fading into memory. Then, they're surprised all over again by the same challenges and weaknesses that plagued their businesses the previous season. This is a *terrible* way to run a business, and it's not how great teams and all-star players prepare. If you and your wife want to experience new growth next season, the time to prepare is *now*.

Preparation paves the way for success.

TRANSITIONING BETWEEN SEASONS

You and your wife should never close out a period in her business without looking ahead to what you need to know/do/prepare for the upcoming season. No business season should exist in isolation; it should always be informed by the one behind and informing the one ahead. By *season*, I'm not necessarily talking about an entire year either. I'm talking about the individual rhythms of the business that we discussed at the start of this section. I'm also talking about the new opportunities and challenges that pop up every time your wife levels up in her business by achieving a new rank. As you and she see one season drawing to a close, you have to be intentional about creating space to talk about what's coming up next.

Beckie and I have had this conversation several times, and we've helped many other couples through it, as well. To keep it super simple, I suggest focusing the discussion around two key actions: *defining* reality and *embracing* reality.

Defining Reality

The first part of the conversation should be focused on defining the reality of what took place in the previous/current season and identifying what will be different in the next. Basically, you need to look back *and* look ahead at the same time. In my soccer days, that meant examining my strengths and weaknesses from the current season and seeing where I needed to improve for the next one. If I hadn't taken my coach's advice and focused on a few key skill areas and my general fitness, I would not have been chosen to be a captain. And, to be blunt, I wouldn't have *deserved* to be a captain. If I wasn't willing to put in some effort between seasons, I didn't deserve the chance to lead the team. My coach helped me define reality by showing me—sometimes in painful detail—where I screwed up and what areas I needed to work on. He didn't do that to hurt me; he did it to make me a better player and a better leader.

In your wife's network-marketing business, this means setting aside time in each season to evaluate what went well, what went poorly, and how you can improve together. It also means tracking the momentum of the current season and identifying specific ways to maximize one season's growth for exponential impact in the next. *Reality* here also means looking at how well the business is fitting into your family and personal goals. It's a time to reexamine and possibly adjust the intentional imbalance you and your wife have agreed on. If you see that the time she spent on the business in one season simply wasn't enough to reach the goals you set together, then you need to have an honest talk about what needs to change. Does she need to commit more time to the business, or do you two need to adjust your shared goals? If something simply isn't working this season, it's dumb to assume it'll magically start working the next season without some tweaking.

This is a critical discussion for your wife's business and for the general health of your relationship. Don't shortchange this step!

Embracing Reality

The next step is pretty obvious, but it's shocking how many couples I've seen fall apart here. Once you define the reality of the current and upcoming seasons, you've got to actually *embrace* the reality of what's coming—and that's not always going to be good news. Embracing reality means facing the challenges head-on. So, say them out loud, acknowledge them, write them down—do whatever you need to do to keep these things from taking you by surprise in the next season as you and your wife work toward your ultimate win.

Embracing reality means facing the challenges head-on.

Don't get overwhelmed with the challenges, though. Embracing reality also means opening your arms to all the incredible opportunities coming your way. If your wife has built momentum in the current season, dream big about where that momentum will take you. Embrace the rewards that will come as the result of her continued hard work and planning. Celebrate how you two will push past limitations, increase income, and grow closer together as you work as a team. If you're doing everything we've discussed in this book so far, your big win is coming; it's inevitable. Embrace the reality of her continued success!

DIG FIRST

There's an ancient Chinese proverb that's loosely translated as, "Dig the well before you are thirsty." That is great advice to live by. If you can anticipate early on what you'll need (and need to do) in the next season, you'll be prepared to keep the momentum going from one season to the next. That's how you experience exponential growth year over year instead of repeating the same level of growth every year. Stephen Covey, author of *The 7 Habits of Highly Effective People*,[7] once said, "Some people say they have twenty years' experience, when, in reality, they only have one year's experience repeated twenty times."[8] Don't repeat the same level of success year over year. Take the time to prepare for next season so you can continue to actually *grow* this business instead of simply *working* this business.

SECTION 3 WRAP-UP

Great job wrapping up another section. We're more than halfway to the finish line! Before we move onto this chapter's action step, let's do a quick flyover of what we learned in this section. First, we discussed the importance of learning the seasons and rhythms of your wife's business. This is one of the most important things you can do to support her business and protect your marriage from constant frustration. Second, we saw how network marketing requires a healthy dose of self-accountability. Like Beckie says, it's an easy business to do and an easy business *not* to do! Third, I challenged you to support your wife in the grind, the weeks or months when the business isn't as fun or exciting and when momentum grinds to a halt. Fourth, we

---

7   Stephen Covey, *The 7 Habits of Highly Effective People* (New York: Simon & Schuster, 2013).

8   Richie Norton, "Happier: The One Secret to Lasting Joy (Implement Immediately)." Medium, December 27, 2017, Accessed February 22, 2019, https://medium.com/@richienorton/happier-the-one-secret-to-lasting-joy-implement-immediately-ebf042869ede.

covered what it takes for your wife to level up in this business and to push past whatever may have gotten her stuck. And finally, in this chapter, I showed you how important it is to always have one eye on the season behind and one on the season ahead.

Now that you have a better understanding of what it takes to build and grow a network-marketing business, it's time to spend a few chapters digging into some of the ups and downs network marketers face in their businesses and how you can help your wife through them all. We'll do that in the next section: No One's Undefeated.

ACTION STEP

The action step for this chapter is to simply identify when the next season of your wife's business will begin. That should be easy if you've done the other action steps for this section. Once you and your wife identify what the next season will be and when it will start, have the two-step discussion—*defining* reality and *embracing* reality—outlined in this chapter to prepare for what's coming. Then you can support your wife as she finishes strong in the current season and prepares well for the next one!

SPOTLIGHT ON SUCCESS

Jon and Jenifer McCann
Color Street, National Executive Director
and Presidential Team Member

My wife, Jen, was a full-time teacher when our second son was born. We had a less-than-ideal childcare situation at the time, and I could see the stress it put on her when she had to leave our boys every morning. She had already dabbled in direct sales, but we took a closer look at her network-marketing company as a way for her to possibly leave her teaching position. Giving up her full-time job in an esteemed school district was one of the first tough decisions we had to make together. I helped her see the benefits of leaving the school, and we worked together to find solutions for all the "what if?" scenarios we could think of. After a million conversations and hours of planning, we decided to take the leap.

Jen did well for a year and a half, but we struggled with the company she worked with. Even though she was successful, they didn't value her leadership and told her outright that she didn't have the skills to handle a larger team. It was hard for me to watch the impact this had on her confidence. We talked a lot about other options, and she eventually found a new opportunity with Color Street. Right away, I knew she'd blow it out of the water.

She worked on both businesses for a few months, but her fast advancement through Color Street's ranks eventually forced her to make a decision: she had to pick one company and give it everything she had. We talked through it together, and I stressed how much I liked Color Street. They seemed to truly value her and see all the great things in her that I did. So, that's the one she chose. From that point on, we worked on the business together. We went on dates devoted to discussing growing her Color Street business, and we talked about how great it was to work with a company so closely aligned with our own values. Her business took off, her confidence went through the roof, she got to stay home with our boys, and all the work we did together brought us closer as a couple. Doing this thing together was a win-win all the way around!

SECTION 4

NO ONE'S UNDEFEATED

CHAPTER 16

NOT IF, BUT WHEN

NOW THAT I'VE SOLD YOU ON THE MASSIVE UPSIDE OF NETWORK marketing and given you some tools to support your wife as she builds a successful business, I'd love to tell you that it's all downhill from here. I'd love to tell you that every day, every week, and every month will be better than the one before. I'd love to tell you that all she'll do from this point on is climb, climb, climb! I'd really *love* to tell you all that... but I can't. The truth is, network marketing can be a roller-coaster ride filled with the highest of highs and the lowest of lows.

I'll never forget finding Beckie crying in the backyard one Friday afternoon. It was the last day of the month, and I've already told you how difficult that day can be for network marketers. I had just gotten home and didn't see her in the house. I looked out the window and saw her sitting alone in the grass. After greeting my kids, I walked out the back door to say hey to my wife and to start, I hoped, another fabulous Farrant weekend.

Didn't Happen

As I walked up to Beckie, I could tell she was crying. *Weeping*, actually. She was more upset than I'd seen her in a long time. I sat down next to her and asked what was wrong. I wasn't sure what she'd say—no husband likes to come home from work and find his wife balled up and crying! She looked up and told me she might be finished with her business for good. Beckie explained that as she was closing out her month that afternoon, she realized she had fallen short of some important monthly goals. Despite her hard work all month, she would end the month by actually *dropping* a rank in her business. This had never happened before; after a year of blasting past her goals like a rocket, she was now taking a step backward. And she was not taking it well.

I convinced her to get off the grass and join me in the hammock. As we swung, she told me she felt like a failure. She was crushed, saying she was letting her team down and that she wasn't sure she was good enough to lead them. She even questioned if she had what it takes to keep progressing in the business. I had never seen her like this before. Beckie is a strong, independent, rockstar entrepreneur! I had seen her crush goals in everything she ever tried to do. But here she was, laying with me in a hammock, questioning everything

It isn't enough to celebrate her wins and challenge her in the day-to-day operations; I had to be ready to support her through her worst days.

about her business and leadership ability. We rocked back and forth for about an hour as I spoke life back into my wife and gave her a safe, quiet place to unload all her pent-up emotions.

Of course, Beckie got her legs back under her pretty quickly and exceeded her goals for the next month. That "hammock day" stuck with us, though. It was a wake-up call for both of us that this is a difficult business full of new challenges every month. As a business owner, Beckie learned that every month gives her a fresh start and new opportunities to win or lose. And, as a husband, I learned that how I respond in the trying times makes a huge impact not only in our marriage but also on her business and bottom line. I saw that how *I* react to her losses will be a critical part of her long-term success. It isn't enough to celebrate her wins and challenge her in the day-to-day operations; I had to be ready to support her through her worst days. And you have to do the same for your wife.

I'M OVER IT!

If you had asked Beckie what she thought about network marketing that day in our backyard, she would have said (pretty bluntly), "I'm over it." I'm sure that wasn't the only day she felt *over it*—over the struggles, over the disappointments, over doing such hard work, over working extra hours, and over the mixed bag of personalities on her team. If your wife hasn't had one of these moments yet, you better believe the day is coming. Every woman who has ever built a successful network-marketing business has felt *over it* at some point—usually immediately after a devastating loss or irritating setback. No business owner has ever had an undefeated season. The losses *will* happen, so we as husbands must be ready to help her navigate the losses that have the potential to make or break her business.

What we *feel* is often driven by what we *expect*.

What causes the "I'm over it" moment? You might think it's just a natural reaction to a bad day/week/month, but I think it's more than that. I don't think it's *just* about a loss; I think the real problem lies in our preparation—or lack of preparation—for the loss in the first place. What we *feel* is often driven by what we *expect*. If we never expect a problem, we'll always be shocked and devastated when one pops up. However, if we understand that even the most successful businesses are often built upon a pile of non-fatal failures, we won't be caught off guard when we feel overwhelmed, disappointed, insecure, or unsure of what to do next. When we go into the business expecting to have "I'm over it" days, they won't shake our foundations as much when they come up. We'll have the perspective we need to see them for what they are: minor annoyances on our way to success. Like the great Babe Ruth once said, "Every strike brings me closer to the next home run."

For your wife, this means understanding that some sales will fall through, some people will say no, and some months will be worse than the previous one. At some point, it will probably also mean taking a step backward in rank as she regroups after a big loss. For you, as her husband and supporter, "I'm over it" days are opportunities to show your wife how much you believe in her. When I found Beckie crying in the backyard, she didn't need me to give her an hour's worth of business advice; she needed me to sit quietly with her as she wept and to speak encouraging words about *who she is*—not tactical ideas about *what she should do*. That's a mistake a lot of husbands I know have made, and it's resulted in the swift end to many promising network-marketing businesses. I don't want your wife's business to be one of them!

PREPARING FOR SETBACKS

Throughout this book, I've tried to give you tactical tips and tools you can use to prepare yourself for all the ins and outs of supporting your wife in her business. Right now, I can't give a numbered list of tried-and-true tricks for preparing for your wife's "I'm over it" moments. Honestly, you're going to have some unique "I'm over it" moments of your own to figure out! What I *can* do, however, is give you a few questions to consider. Review these carefully and take a few minutes to honestly answer each one for yourself.

Do You See Network Marketing as an Easy, Painless Way to Build Wealth?

If you're still looking for a get-rich-quick scheme, go back and read the first section of the book again. Remind yourself as often as necessary that there is no such thing as get rich quick. And, if there was, network marketing would not be it. Everyone who sticks with this business and ultimately finds success in it knows that it's hard, time-consuming, often-frustrating work. If you and your wife want easy money, look somewhere else. Network marketing isn't the answer, and the longer you hold onto the belief that network marketing is easy, the more you'll set yourself up for a painful reality check in the future.

The longer you hold onto the belief that network-marketing is easy, the more you'll set yourself up for a painful reality check in the future.

Do You Believe There Will Be Setbacks?

Beckie is the most dynamic entrepreneur I've ever met. If anyone could have gone directly from point A to point B in this business without any missteps or backtracking, it would have been her. However, she and I have had several hard reminders that nobody—*nobody*—has a perfect track record in network marketing. Keep the roller-coaster image in your mind: sometimes the business takes off like a rocket, sometimes it takes a deep dive, sometimes it spirals, and sometimes it even moves backward. Just remember that it's all part of the ride. Nobody gets on Disney's Space Mountain expecting it to be as flat and easygoing as the monorail!

**Are You Prepared to Love and Support
Your Wife through the Setbacks?**
This isn't a network-marketing question; it's a marriage question. Think about a difficult time when you've stepped up to love your wife through a hard time. What was your instinct? How did you support her through the loss? What impact did your reaction in that situation have on your marriage over the long term?

Your wife takes her business seriously. She probably went into it with excitement, full of passion and huge expectations. So, when the business hits a snag—and it will—she's probably going to take the hit pretty hard. When that happens, do not dismiss it as "her silly business thing." Don't write it off as "no big deal," and, at the other extreme, don't encourage her to throw in the towel. Your job in the "I'm over it" moments is to stay calm, give her a shoulder to lean on, offer a safe place to vent her frustrations, and simply love her however you would in any other hard situation. This business sometimes has a way of sucking the life out of the best of us, so be ready to speak words of life back into her when she needs it. I'm sure you've done that in a hundred other ways, so this is something you should already know how to do.

GET BACK UP

Hall of Fame coach Vince Lombardi once said, "It's not whether you get knocked down, it's whether you get back up." It's true in sports, and it's certainly true in business. Your wife *will* get knocked down. It's *going* to happen, so get ready for it. The real question isn't, "Will she have setbacks?" but rather, "How can I help her get back up when she gets knocked down?"

Throughout the next few chapters, we're going to explore how to support our wives in the losses, struggles, setbacks, and "I'm over it" moments. These aren't just trying and emotional times; they're also likely to be the key make-or-break moments in your wife's business. If she (and you) can't get past these obstacles, you two will never achieve the big win you've set for her business. What you do and say on these bad days will make all the difference when she's crying and wondering if it's time to give up. You (and maybe you alone) have the power to lift

What you do and say on these bad days will make all the difference

her up and give her the strength to get up, push through the pain, and continue moving forward in her business. Beckie never would have achieved the big win we set for her business if she stayed balled up in the grass, and neither will your wife.

So, get down there with her and remind her what makes you the best husband, partner, friend, and encourager she could ever have!

ACTION STEP

For this chapter's action step, I want you to write or type the following sentences:

1. We will experience losses and setbacks while trying to build this business.
2. We will have "I'm over it" moments.
3. I will navigate these moments with an attitude of love, learning, and encouragement.
4. We will not quit because of any loss, setback, or "I'm over it" moment.

Review these statements regularly. Say them out loud and commit them to memory. Pull them out whenever your wife is having a bad day in the business, and gently remind her that you both knew there would be some setbacks as she works to build something you both can (and will) be proud of.

CHAPTER 17

LEARN FROM A LOSS

I TOLD YOU ABOUT ANGELA AND ERIC BACK IN CHAPTER 7.
Remember that Angela is the one who didn't fully understand her
company's compensation plan and missed out on a $500 bonus
because she didn't structure her sales properly. That was a huge loss
for their family, but it wasn't completely Angela's fault. Eric, who
had a natural gift for numbers, hadn't been helping her. He failed
to get involved and learn the comp plan, and he never offered to
lend his knack for accounting to her business. When we left off with
them in Chapter 7, they were at a fork in the road. Now, let's see
what happened next.

That mistake was a gut-check moment for Angela and Eric.
The situation caused them to reevaluate what they were doing, how
they were doing it, and if they should even bother doing the business at all. That $500 screwup was the kind of loss that could have
easily caused Angela to quit the business entirely. It's also the kind
of mistake that could have caused Eric to poke fun at his wife over
what he might have seen as incompetence or carelessness. In many
situations like this, the business comes to a screeching halt either due
to the wife's frustration or the husband's mocking. It stinks, but I've
seen it play out that way several times. Thankfully, though, that's not
what happened with Angela and Eric.

Beckie and I met with them to talk through the mistake. The four of us discussed what happened and what they could learn from it. They realized this situation was a huge learning opportunity—one they certainly wouldn't forget anytime soon. As a result of their mistake and our conversation, Angela and Eric were motivated to learn how to maximize the comp plan and business structure. More importantly, they agreed the best way to win would be to work together, with each bringing their strengths and giftedness to the table.

Learn from your losses.

Adding Eric's strengths with numbers, strategic thinking, and creating processes took Angela's business to the next level. As I sit here writing this, Angela just completed her biggest sales month ever and they are about to get the biggest paycheck either of them has ever received! Her success has also enabled her to level up a few times, and she hit a huge rank this month. Her business is booming, and the couple can't imagine what their lives would be like at this point if they had given up after that $500 mistake. Because she stuck with it and they used that experience to address some broken things in her business, she's made that $500 back many times over. That's what I call learning from a loss!

DON'T SCREW UP YOUR SCREWUP

Every team experiences some losses. The best running backs will fumble. The best NBA player will brick a game-losing jump shot. Even Tiger Woods in his prime didn't win every tournament. In the previous chapter, I told you to expect problems in your wife's business. If you weren't paying attention then, let me reiterate: problems aren't a matter of if, but when. Something's going to happen that will shake her (and your) faith in the business. Sometimes, it will be beyond anyone's control; other times, it will be her fault. That's okay. It is going to happen. I'd encourage you to say that out loud a dozen times: *It is going to happen.*

The thing that separates great athletes from average players is what they *learn* from their losses. The same is true for business builders. If you and your wife want to build something you can both be proud of, something that will lead you to the big win you've identified for yourselves, then you've got to be ready, willing, and able to learn from your losses. It's not enough to simply brace yourself and expect them to happen; you have to face them head-on so you can take something useful out of the experience.

When the loss comes, one of the most important commitments you can make is to say, "I will not screw up my screwup." That is, you won't screw up the way you *handle* your screwup. It's one thing to make a mistake like structuring sales the wrong way and missing out on a $500 bonus. It's a much bigger mistake, though, to react to that kind of loss by blowing up in anger at your wife and allowing her—even *encouraging* her—to quit because of it. We *all* make mistakes, but we make it exponentially worse when we screw up the way we handle our screwups.

"I will not screw up my screwup."

Instead, we need to accept the fact that losses are our best opportunities for growth. Looking back over my life, marriage, and career, I can say without hesitation that the most important lessons I've ever learned have been the result of some painful, embarrassing failures. At the heart of each of those failures was a decision I had to make: *Will this fool me or fuel me?* Would I let those mistakes and missteps trick me into giving up something that could lead to incredible benefits, or would I use those screwups as fuel to learn bigger and better lessons about something I really cared about? I haven't gotten it right every time, but Beckie and I have made the conscious decision to look for the lesson in every loss. It's not easy, but it's always worth it.

HOW TO LEARN FROM A LOSS

If you have even a passing interest in sports, I'm sure you've heard about Michael Jordan's early days in basketball. He famously failed to earn a spot on his high school varsity team as a sophomore. Instead of allowing that loss to define him, sending him home defeated and beating his basketball dreams into the dirt, he used it as fuel. He practiced more. He worked out harder. He spent even more time perfecting his game. Obviously, looking back over his incredible career, we can see that all that hard work paid off. But it started with a failure, and it was peppered with more failures throughout his time on the basketball court. Jordan later reflected, "I've missed more than nine hundred shots in my career. I've lost almost three hundred games. Twenty-six times, I've been trusted to take the game-winning shot and missed. I've failed over and over and over again in my life. And *that* is why I succeed."[9]

> **You can't fix what you won't see as broken.**

If you and your wife want to "be like Mike," you've got to figure out how to learn from a loss and not let it define or discourage you. Here are four steps to help you get started:

Embrace the Loss

You can't fix what you won't see as broken. Angela made a mistake by not organizing her sales correctly and maximizing the compensation plan. Eric made a mistake by not using his gifts and experience to help her with something she wasn't comfortable with. They both screwed up. Great! It happens. Face it. Embrace it. Admit it. Deal with it. Discuss it. Evaluate what went wrong and how you can learn from it. Allow it to add fuel to your business-building fire. Figure out ways to avoid that same problem in the future. That's what Eric and

9 "Forbes Quotes: Thoughts on the Business of Life," *Forbes*, accessed January 3, 2019, https://www.forbes.com/quotes/11194/.

Angela did, that's what Beckie and I have done, and that's what you and your wife *must* do if you want to win in this business.

Own Your Part

Most people tend to either *over-own* or *under-own* their responsibility in the face of a mistake. If you are an over-owner, you probably take way too much blame than you should when something goes wrong. You may beat yourself up over it and feel a mountain of shame and embarrassment pressing down on you. If you are an under-owner, you may shift all the blame to other people, driving them crazy with your excuses and rationalizations for why something wasn't your fault instead of accepting the fact that you're human and you sometimes screw up.

Be honest with yourself: which one are you? If you don't know, ask your wife. I *promise* it won't take her long to set you straight. Learning from a loss means owning your part of the responsibility. The key phrase here is *your part*. That means not avoiding the blame and not taking everyone else's blame on yourself.

Pay Attention to the Pain

Losses are painful! I *hate* losing, whether it's in sports, business, board games (Monopoly, anyone?), or anything else. Losses in network marketing can look like missing out on a bonus because you didn't understand the comp plan well enough, dropping down a rank because you slacked off for a month or two, or losing a customer because you failed to follow through the way you were taught. I've seen all these play out many times with all the network marketers I know, and nobody likes dealing with these kinds of setbacks. But, before you dismiss, bury, or run from the pain caused by a loss, ask yourself *why*. Why did you or your wife mess up? Why did you get a result you don't like? Why didn't you see this coming?

Let the *why* question drive you back to the *fruit* and *root* issues we covered in Chapter 14. Pay attention to the pain and dig down through it until you figure out the real root issue. Have the courage to ask yourself, *Was this a simple oversight I need to learn from or is there a deeper reality I need to uncover in my life?*

Leverage the Experience
Finally, you must find a way to squeeze *some* value out of the loss. Every great business builder figures out how to leverage their losses for future success. Ask yourself, *What's the lesson to be learned here? What caused this mistake, and what can I/we do to prevent it in the future?*

Optimistic people may say, "When life hands you lemons, make lemonade." That's a nice thought, but it's not what a good entrepreneur would say. If you and your wife are serious about building a successful business, you need a mindset that says, "When life hands you lemons, make a lemonade stand." That way, you aren't just squeezing a

> **"When life hands you lemons, make a lemonade stand."**

moment of joy out of the ordeal (pun intended); you're using the lesson to build a business.

I get it. Nobody likes to fall flat on their face, especially when the game is on the line. But people who get back up, who fight through the sting of a loss and choose to get some value out of it, are the ones who win over the long term. When you and your wife master this hard lesson, you'll start to build an amazing business and future together.

DON'T EAT YOUR PUKE

There's a biblical proverb that says, "As a dog returns to its vomit, so a fool repeats his foolishness."[10] That's a nice way of saying that repeating a stupid mistake is as dumb and gross as a dog eating its

10 Proverbs 26:11, NLT.

own puke. But that's exactly what we do when we fail to—or *refuse* to—learn from our losses. One of the worst things we can do while trying to build a successful network-marketing business is to screw up and then ignore it. That just sets us up to repeat the same mistake over and over and over again. That kind of laziness will keep your business in a death spiral until you and your wife ultimately give up. You may blame the business model when that happens, but the harsh truth is that you missed out on your big win because you refused to embrace the loss, own your part, pay attention to the pain, and leverage the experience.

Don't be a fool and repeat your foolishness. Learn from the loss so you won't make the same mistake again.

ACTION STEP

Take a few minutes to think through the four steps mentioned in this chapter:

1. Embrace the Loss
2. Own Your Part
3. Pay Attention to the Pain
4. Leverage the Experience

Which of these things is most challenging for you? What could you do to change that so you can maximize the value hiding in every setback?

I'd encourage you to share this chapter with your wife and ask her to identify which of these four steps she most struggles with. When you each know the other's weakest areas, you can work together to safeguard her business from the potential devastation of a big loss.

CHAPTER 18

SAFE AND SOUND

THINGS DIDN'T TURN OUT EXACTLY THE WAY MARSHA HAD HOPED.
Months earlier, she had met a bright and energetic woman named
Christy, and the two hit it off big-time. Marsha was thrilled when
Christy expressed an interest in joining her business; Christy had a
great network of people and a real passion for the product. Marsha
just *knew* Christy would be a key player and would help her achieve
her own business goals. As Marsha got Christy started, the two
discussed Christy's long-term goals and Marsha saw her as a great
fit. But there was a problem: Marsha never asked Christy what *pace*
she wanted to go to achieve her goals. Based on her energy and
outgoing personality, Marsha assumed Christy was going to jump in
at a runner's pace. Christy, on the other hand, just wanted to walk.
She enjoyed the business, but she wasn't in a hurry to reach her goals
and she had other commitments that required her time and attention. The two weren't on the same page, and they were heading for
trouble—a *lot* of trouble.

Based on bad expectations, Marsha placed Christy in a prom-
inent position in her team organization. The truth is, Marsha had
a lot riding on Christy's performance; that's what made Christy's
pace so frustrating. Marsha simply could not understand why she
was moving so slow! As a result, Marsha spent the next two months

pushing Christy too hard. Finally, the ladies hit their breaking point. Christy lashed out at Marsha in a cringeworthy verbal assault. She was *done* with Marsha's endless pushing and prodding, and she was mad at how she thought she was being treated. As a result, Christy set a new business goal: hurt Marsha's business.

Marsha was stunned and spent several weeks trying to apologize, but Christy wouldn't take her calls or respond to her emails. The only time Marsha heard from Christy was through a few pointed text messages designed to hurt Marsha even more. Christy made it clear that she was going to do whatever she could to keep Marsha's business from moving forward. And, because Marsha had placed her in a key spot in her organization, Christy had the power to screw up all of Marsha's goals for a long time.

This is such a dramatic, overblown story that you might think I'm making it up. Nope. This actually happened, and it was devastating to Marsha's business. It held her back for several months and robbed her of the momentum she needed to hit her goals. This was a rare situation when everyone involved lost.

What would you have done if you were Marsha's husband? What would you have said as all this unfolded? I mean, Marsha definitely messed up. This ordeal was her fault, and even though Christy took things way too far, Marsha could have avoided the whole situation by doing a better job onboarding her new team member. As a result, Marsha's husband had to sit through months of drama, lost income, slowed momentum, and emotional outbursts. They also had to figure out how to work around Christy, who was now sitting like a boulder in the middle of Marsha's organization.

Moments like these aren't just about your wife's business, meeting her goals, and keeping her momentum going. As a husband, these kinds of moments are critical for your marriage. They are defining moments in which you'll show your wife whether you are a *safe and sound* person for her to fall back on in times of trouble.

Will you be a *safe* place for her to admit the mistakes she made and a source of encouragement for her in the midst of trouble? Will you give *sound,* helpful advice that will help her learn from the loss without piling on more guilt and judgement? My guess is if you're reading this book, that's what you *want* to do, so let's figure out how to make it happen.

BECOMING A SAFE AND SOUND HUSBAND

Over the past twenty years as a pastor, I've spent thousands of hours helping married couples process, handle, and grow during some really difficult situations. I've worked with couples going through affairs, job losses, sick children, addictions, and worse. Of course, the challenges of building a network-marketing business can't compare to these things, but there are some basic principles that *do* apply to your wife's business. Again, these can be critical times for your marriage, so we need to know how, as husbands, to respond correctly.

When she messes up in her business—when she totally blows it and feels terrible about herself—what you do and say will speak volumes to her.

These situations are perfect opportunities to show love to your wife. This is when you'll show her what you really think about her and how you really feel about her. When she messes up in her business—when she totally blows it and feels terrible about herself—what you do and say will speak volumes to her. You will have the power to make things better or to make them ten times worse. As good men and loving husbands, our job should be to soften the blow, share the burden, and help her let go of her regret and embarrassment. Too many husbands, though, take the opposite approach. Without thinking, they make snide comments or pile on more guilt that only make their wives feel worse about themselves. In fact, I've seen many businesses end at this critical juncture—and the marriages weren't too far behind.

But what if you responded in love? What if you showed her with your words and actions that you love her no matter what, that no business mistake could ever change how much you value her? What if, in these moments, you proved yourself to be a safe and sound place for her to run to? That wouldn't just help the business problem; it would bring a greater unity into your marriage. You could turn a disaster into fuel for strengthening your marriage. But, in order to be this type of husband, you must do three crucial things:

> **No one's words have more of an impact on your wife than yours.**

Realize Your Words Have Weight

No one's words have more of an impact on your wife than yours. I don't care if we're talking about business, relationships, hobbies, intelligence, driving ability, or anything else—your opinion means the most to her (and vice versa). Your words *matter*, so you must be careful how, when, and where you use them. Be patient and wise with your words and try your best to never lash out in a moment of anger or frustration. That kind of response can create a deep wound in your wife when she is at her most vulnerable. An old Chinese proverb says, "If you are patient in one moment of anger, you will escape a hundred days of sorrow." If you've ever suffered through a few rocky weeks of the cold-shoulder treatment after an argument, you know exactly what I'm talking about!

A biblical proverb says, "The tongue has the power of life and death."[11] I really believe that. Your words can speak life into your wife, help her recover from a loss, make her feel better about herself, and undo much of the damage caused by someone else's cruelty. Or,

11 Proverbs 18:21, NIV.

on the other hand, they can speak words of death to her, piling onto her feelings of shame, guilt, fear, and regret. Bottom line: You can make things *better* or *worse*. If you love her, your goal should be to use your words to make things better.

Focus on Her—Not Her Productivity

When your wife goes through a rough patch like this, she doesn't need your backseat driving comments about her business. Do you think Marsha needed her husband to throw her mistake in her face with comments like, "Do you realize how big an impact this mistake is going to have on your business?" or "Good grief, honey. I can't believe you let this happen." No way; she was *living* that mistake and its impact every day. Be extra careful in these conversations to focus on your wife as a person, not on her productivity. Yes, the business may stall a bit. Yes, it may cost her some lost income. Yes, she may have to work harder to get past it. And yes, she already knows all this!

> **Focus on your wife as a person, not on her productivity.**

In these moments, your wife needs some reassurance that you value her as a person, not just as an income earner or source of productivity. She's your *wife*. That should be enough whether she hits all her business goals or not.

Leave the Past in the Past

Time to be real here. One of the worst things a husband can do in *any* situation is bring up his wife's past mistakes. This is absolutely devastating to her and makes her feel more *unsafe* than just about anything. It also shows her that you are incapable of bringing sound advice because you can't get over something that happened months or years ago.

I doubt most husbands mean to throw past mistakes in their wives' faces, but it happens more than you'd think. In network marketing, it generally comes out like, "Not again! I thought for sure you learned your lesson the last time this happened!" Or maybe, "Are you serious? This is the third time you've made this mistake. Do I need to take it over for you?" Seriously, guys...what are we thinking when we do this?

Repeat after me: *When my wife is going through a hard time, even if it's her fault, my goal will be to dignify her and not to destroy her.* If she's blown it, she is already well aware of the screwup, and she is probably already reliving some of her old mistakes too. She definitely does not need you to push the dagger in deeper by bringing up painful things from the past.

You may be thinking, *But Tim, why should I treat my wife this way? She certainly doesn't hesitate to bring up my past mistakes! And she doesn't mind hitting me in the face with her harsh words or talking about how much money I make (or don't make).* Two things here. First of all, I get it. I know it can be hard to be a safe and sound husband when your wife doesn't do the same for you. Second, *get over it*! Stop whining about what she does or doesn't do for you. Be a man and set a good example in your home and in your marriage. Step up and do the right thing no matter what she does. If you stop making excuses, do the right thing, and respond the right way, I bet she'll take notice. She may even follow your lead and change how she responds to you, too. This could be the first step to the two of you becoming safe and sound for *each other*.

WHERE WILL SHE RUN?

After she takes a big hit, your wife will run *somewhere*. It may be to her friends or upline leaders. It might be to a bottle of wine. It could be to a pint of ice cream and a twenty-four-hour Netflix binge. She could run in a hundred different directions. But what if she ran to you instead? What if she knew without a doubt that you were the safest, most loving, most secure place she could go to for comfort?

What if she trusted you to give her the sound advice she needed to fix her mistake and help get back on her feet? How could that change her business? More importantly, how could that change your marriage?

Marriages are built on grace and understanding—two things you demonstrate every time you prove yourself to be a safe and sound place to run.

ACTION STEP

Spend a few minutes today reflecting on the questions below. Jot down a few notes as you honestly answer each one.

1. Are you a safe and sound person for your wife?
2. How do you currently handle a loss in your wife's business? If you're a safe and sound person for her, how do you demonstrate it? If you're not, what does that look like?
3. Based on this chapter, what changes do you need to make in how you respond to losses in your wife's business?

CHAPTER 19

HYPE MAN

SHEILA WAS A BUSINESS BUILDER WITH A LOT OF POTENTIAL. SHE had a great reputation in her community, was extremely outgoing, had a huge circle of friends, and truly believed in the product. Most importantly, she was up to the challenge of building her own business and excited to get started. All signs pointed toward enormous success for Sheila in this business, and any network marketer would have been thrilled to add her to their team. So, with a great deal of excitement and a little bit of nerves, Sheila set up her first few calls to start building her business.

There was only one problem—and that problem's name was Natalie. Natalie was Sheila's sister. The two usually got along and were great friends as well as siblings, so Sheila was anxious to sit down with Natalie and tell her all about the business, her goals, and her passion for the product. She really wanted her sister's support, even if Natalie wasn't interested in joining the business herself. What Sheila got, however, wasn't that. In fact, it was the opposite. After listening for a while, Natalie finally spoke up and said, "You're being so stupid. This is all a complete waste of time, and you're getting your hopes up about something that is never going to work. No one *ever* has any success in these types of businesses. You're just setting yourself up to fail."

That conversation smothered Sheila's business like a wet blanket. It killed her enthusiasm, and it made her question not only her involvement in the business but also her belief in the product itself. Sheila stuck with it and ultimately found success in network marketing, but I know she would have gone further faster if her sister had been building her up instead of tearing her down.

For some reason, network marketing is a lightning rod for criticism. People will say things about network marketing that they'd never say about any other business. If my wife had decided to get a real estate license and start a new business selling houses, I'm sure everyone we know would have been thrilled. They'd have sent cards, emails, and texts congratulating her, and they would have recommended all their friends to her to help build her business. That's not what happened when she decided to start a network-marketing business, however. Because most people don't understand network-marketing and are generally suspicious of it, they tend to dismiss it, question it, mock it, and condescendingly question how anyone could fall for it. The most hurtful and devastating losses in network marketing are often not from the business but from the people outside the business looking in. Even if the business itself is great, family and friends can steal every ounce of satisfaction with their thoughtless, hurtful comments.

As good husbands, what should our response be when we hear the negative and downright mean things people say about our wives' businesses? Do you laugh along with them, poking fun at what your wife is working so hard to accomplish? Do you just let the comments slide past you without giving any reaction at all? Do you get angry and lash out at the other person? What about when your wife is completely wrecked because someone she cares about questions her motives or calls her an idiot for getting started in this business?

We talked about the importance of being your wife's *corner man* in Chapter 10. Now, it's time to look at another crucial role

you can (and should) play in her business. To take another role out
of the boxing playbook, let's look at what it means to be your wife's
hype man.

BE HER DON KING

I am just old enough to remember when professional boxers had
hype men. Sometimes, the hype man was as famous as the boxing
champ himself! The most successful boxing hype man of all time had
to be Don King. This guy was *crazy*. Everything about him demanded
your attention—his hair, his voice, his style, his entire persona was
engineered to evoke energy and enthusiasm. He had the kind of
swagger and confidence that made you believe his fighters were the
best in the world. And yes, before you start sending me emails about
him, I know there were a lot of questions about Don King's business
practices, and I certainly don't agree with
many of the personal life choices he made.
But, when it comes down to purely hyping
a boxer and promoting a fight, it doesn't get
any better than Don King.

How much confidence would it give
your wife if she knew you were her own,
personal hype man? How would it feel
for her—in the face of someone's criticism,

How much confidence would it give your wife if she knew you were her own, personal hype man?

insults, or doubt—to know for a fact that you had her back? To know
that you were there going ahead of her, cheering her on, preparing
the crowds, offering encouragement, and getting her amped up for
her next appointment? To know that you aren't on the side of the
naysayers talking bad about her and tearing her down? It sounds so
obvious, but I'm shocked that *every* husband isn't his wife's biggest
hype man! Sadly, though, some women can have a hard day and then
come home knowing their *biggest* critic is there waiting on them.
Don't be that guy! You want to be the safe and sound person, the

partner, the teammate, the corner man—the hype man! That's what she wants you to be and, more importantly, that's who she *needs* you to be.

You will show your wife what you really think about her and her business by what you say and how you say it. If you laugh it off when someone calls her foolish for working toward her goals, she'll know you're laughing *her* off too. If you join in when people are making fun of her, she'll know you're making fun of her too. But, if you shut down friends' criticisms and boldly support your wife and her goals to other people, she'll know for sure that you really do support her. No one wants a hype man who caves the first time someone says a bad word about his boxer. If you're serious about supporting your wife and her business, then you've got to shout that support boldly with your words and actions in every situation.

You need to be the Don King of your wife's business. That means being 100 percent committed to her success, telling everyone how awesome she is and how proud you are of her, speaking up for her when others are putting her down, and caring more about what she thinks than what anyone else thinks. You need to be ready, willing, and able to embarrass yourself if that's what it takes to show the world how awesome your wife is!

THREE CRAPPY TRUTHS FOR THE HYPE MAN

Once you commit to choose your wife over everyone else and to support her over anyone else's jokes or objections, you'll need to embrace three crappy truths about other people. I don't want to come across as judgmental or condescending here, but these are three indisputable facts I've learned through our personal experiences in network marketing and through helping several other couples grow their businesses. None of these three things should be surprising, however. The only real surprise should be that people can actually act like this.

People's Cheers Are Conditional

People will cheer for your wife when it serves them. People will cheer for your wife when they understand and approve of what she's doing. But the moment they don't like or understand something, their cheers will quickly turn into *boos*. We talked about this a bit in Chapter 6, where I made the point that even the most diehard fans will turn on their team at the drop of a dime. And, when they do, things get ugly. You've seen this at every sporting event you've ever attended. When the home team is winning, the crowd is cheering like crazy. However, the first time a player screws up, all those cheers immediately turn into *boos*. Sometimes, the booing is even louder than the cheering ever was!

You cannot base your level of support on the size of the crowd or the volume of their cheers.

You cannot base your level of support on the size of the crowd or the volume of their cheers. Your support can only be based on your wife. Crowds are fickle, so your love and commitment to your wife must be the firm foundation your support is built on. Don't let anyone *boo* you out of supporting her and what she's trying to accomplish. Remember, you're her hype man. If she's only hearing *boos*, it's your job to turn those *boos* into cheers. And, if the crowd is already cheering, it's your job to make them cheer even louder!

Her Success Intimidates Others

Even if people assume the worst at the start of the business, you'd assume most of them would come around after she has some success. Isn't that what normally happens in every other industry? The more houses a new real estate agent sells, for example, the more people trust her and the more confident they are in referring their friends to her to help grow her business even more. That's just not the case in network marketing—at least not in my experience. As I've said, the more success Beckie achieved, the more people talked bad about her. Some of the worst naysayers appeared *after* she got successful! I'm afraid to say the same will be true for your wife. Sure, she'll win over some early critics, but others will say things like, "It looks okay now, but let's just see how things look a year from now. I bet she's not even working the business by then." Or maybe, "Enjoy it while you can! This whole business is built on a house of cards, and it will come crashing down soon enough!" The worst may be, "I can't believe she's conned that many people to join her. She must be the best liar in the business."

Success intimidates the unsuccessful.

I have no patience for this or for the people spreading this garbage. The ugly truth is that success intimidates the unsuccessful. When people say your wife can't win in this business, what they're really saying is that *they* cannot win in this business. They're viewing your wife's ability through the lens of their inability, and it makes the whole thing appear suspicious to them. Believe in what your wife *can* do, and don't waste your time listening to the critiques of those who *can't*.

Hurt People Hurt People

My years as a pastor have shown me a universal constant: hurt people hurt people. That is, people who have suffered a tragic loss or are simply discouraged by their lack of success can become the loudest critics of all. It's not that they really think the worst about your wife; it's that they've come to believe the worst about themselves. They've been beaten up and tossed around by life, and they can't separate their own pain and loss from someone else's apparent success. Their perspective is skewed, and it causes them to see the whole world—including your wife—off-kilter. Very sad, but very true.

HYPE MAN, NOT LITIGATOR

As the hype man, you'll be on the front lines facing all the criticism people throw at your wife. And, if you're a confrontational type of guy, you may be tempted to argue back at all the objections people give you. Trust me on this: it's a waste of time. The problem is, we can never really know where someone's coming from. We can only hear *what* they say; we usually can't hear *why* they're saying it. If they're speaking out of pain, I don't want to make their situation worse. And, if they're criticizing simply because they're a jerk, I know I'll never convince them of the merits of network marketing anyway. It's not my job to be Beckie's litigator, to argue every point in favor of network marketing and to systematically destroy everyone else's objections. No, it's my job in those moments to simply be her hype man, to believe in her ability more than I believe in the foolish things other people say, and to talk her up as loud and long as possible. That's what Don King would do!

It's time for an honest self-evaluation. Spend a few minutes reflecting on the question: *How good of a hype man have I been for my wife?* Think through times when you've had the chance to hype her or hurt her. Then, rate yourself as a hype man on a scale of one to ten. Finally, answer the following questions:

① How pleased are you with the rating you gave yourself?
② Is this the hype man your wife deserves?
③ In what specific ways can you become a better hype man, and how will you put this into action?

CHAPTER 20

DON'T BE A QUITTER

ABBY WAS AN INCH AWAY FROM HER BREAKING POINT. SHE HAD been building her business for six months before hitting a soul-crushing dry spell. Things had gone pretty well for her all spring as she got ramped up, but then . . . summer happened. I've said before that summer is usually a slow season (at least for Beckie's business), but Abby's summer business wasn't just slow; it was standing still. Discounts didn't work. Calls went unanswered. Emails disappeared into the black hole of the Internet. Finally, after weeks of trying to set up a meeting with a potential business builder from church, she got an appointment for a coffee meeting one Friday morning at 10:00 a.m. This meeting was all she needed to keep her hopes up. *I can handle slow business*, she thought. *I just can't handle no business.* With nothing else lined up, Abby set her sights on this one meeting and was determined to make the most of it.

She was so excited that Friday that she arrived thirty minutes early. She had her presentation ready and talking points memorized, and she had even prepared a few charts and slides to show her friend on her tablet as they talked. She sat there brimming with excitement as she waited. And waited. And waited. At 10:20 a.m., the painful realization shot through her like a bullet. *She's not coming.* Totally deflated and defeated, Abby gathered her things, took the last swig of her peppermint mocha, and went home. She quit the business the next day.

I'd love to say this kind of situation is rare in network marketing, but we all know it's not. I've said over and over that this is a valid business with huge potential, but it's certainly not easy. It takes time and hard work. Perhaps even more than that, though, it requires thick skin. People *will* say no. People *will* flake out on meetings. People *will* think your wife is nuts for trying some "network-marketing thing." I won't sugarcoat it for you; all of this and more *will happen.* Ignoring the inevitable hiccups and hardships will only make things worse.

SUCCESSFUL PEOPLE DON'T QUIT

When Jerry Jones bought the Dallas Cowboys in 1989, he was buying a boatload of problems. He paid a whopping $140 million for the team—the first NFL team to sell for more than $100 million—but the Cowboys were struggling financially. They had a great tradition and diehard fans (it *was* Texas, after all), but the Dallas Cowboys as a business was *losing* $1 million a month. Jones had an uphill battle from his very first day as an owner, but he also had a dream. He had a vision in his head—his big win—for where he wanted the team to go, and he was prepared to put in the time and hard work required to get there. And, of course, he wasn't afraid to face the trouble they were in. He knew that leaning into the mess was the only way to get through it. Thirty years later, all his hard work has paid off. As of September 2018, the Cowboys were the most valuable franchise in the NFL for the twelfth year in a row, valued at $5 billion![12] How did that happen? Because Jerry Jones didn't quit.

12 Darren Rovel, "Forbes: Cowboys most valuable NFL team for 12th year in row," Forbes.com, September 20, 2018, http://www.espn.com/espnw/sports/article/24742979/forbes-magazine-dallas-cowboys-5b-again-most-valuable.

I've been blessed to talk to and work with several successful network-marketing women over the years. There's not one specific *type* of person who's more or less successful in building a business. Everyone is different and brings different skills and weaknesses to the table. Some of the network-marketing superstars I know are crazy, outgoing party people. Others are more reserved and prefer a quiet coffee shop over a booming dance floor. Some see everything through a relational lens, and others struggle with one-on-one conversations with new people. Some started the business as customers who fell in love with the product, while others went straight for the business opportunity. Every one of these things describes someone I know in the business.

Anyone who ever achieved anything of significance faced intense struggles on their way to victory.

While there are many differences, I have found that every single successful network-marketing pro I know has gone through the exact same experience at some point. Over and over, these women have told me:

1. Even though there were moments of incredible joy and fun, building their businesses wasn't easy.
2. They experienced several significant, painful losses along the way.
3. They faced many key defining moments when they truly wanted to quit.
4. They hung in there and ultimately refused to give up.

Anyone who ever achieved anything of significance faced intense struggles on their way to victory. You and your wife are no different. If you stick with this business, you're going to have some difficult days ahead—days when one or both of you want to throw in the towel. However, quitting the business also means quitting the big win you identified early on. I don't want you and your wife to give up on your goals, so let's take a minute to prepare for the day when everything inside you wants to say, "I quit."

FACE YOUR LOSSES

To build a successful network-marketing business without giving in to the pressure to quit, you and your wife must be prepared to face the losses. From what I've seen by watching dozens of women crush their business goals, I suggest you do this in two key ways:

Step into the Struggle

I know the last few chapters haven't been all sunshine and rainbows. We've talked about struggles, emotional ups and downs, losses, and how to be a safe place for your wife to turn to when her business goes sideways. If someone *only* reads this section of the book, they'd get a pretty bleak picture of network marketing! Of course, the business has a huge upside, but the last thing I want to do is sell you some warm and fuzzy dream about a network-marketing empire fueled by unicorns and pixie dust. That's not real—and neither is a vision of network marketing completely free of pain and loss. Any goal worth pursuing comes with its share of struggles, from weight loss to getting out of debt. If everything worthwhile came easily, we'd all be fabulously wealthy, famous, and ripped. But we're not.

Our culture has fallen so in love with comfort that we spend our days meandering through life with our eyes glued to our little flashing screens looking for nonstop distractions to prevent us from *accidentally* seeing anything that brings us down. Forget *facing* the struggle; most of us go out of our way to hide from the struggle altogether. Our top goal in every decision is usually, "Avoid pain and maximize pleasure." That's the mindset that leads to thirty-year-old *children* living in their parents' basements with an endless stream of Netflix, video games, and gadgets in front of them and a huge pile of credit card bills, unmet expectations, and broken dreams behind them. They'd rather focus on the flashy crap that distracts them than spend one minute dealing with the hard realities of life that could actually *take* them somewhere!

If this describes you, then I'm calling you out. Man up! Have the guts to turn away from the distractions and face your struggle. Stop losing yourself in beer, football, and Xbox. **Stop making excuses and start stepping into the struggle that comes with doing something significant!** Stop consuming yourself with your kids' activities instead of leaning into the hard work of reaching your family goals. Stop making excuses and start stepping into the struggle that comes with doing something significant! This isn't a network-marketing lesson; this is a life lesson! This is something that will change your marriage, your family, your business, your spiritual life, your relationships, and your finances. The key to stopping the slide into becoming twenty-first-century zombies is to turn away from the drool-inducing appeasements of life and deal with the things that must be dealt with.

Don't Follow Your Feelings

Repeat after me: Feelings are not facts. That is a bitter pill for many people to swallow, but it is a crucial fact of life. Too often, we allow our feelings to drag us around by the nose. We make bad, ultimately unfulfilling decisions because we place too much emphasis on what *feels* good. Your wife doesn't *feel* good when someone stands her up for a business chat, and it certainly doesn't *feel* good when a potential builder tells her to take a hike. If she were going by feelings alone, she'd quit the first time anyone made her feel bad about her business. Just think about how good it would feel, what a relief it would be, to bring a swift and immediate end to the pain of a bad business week by throwing your hands up and saying, "That's it! I'm out!"

But there is a huge difference between what you *know* and what you *feel*. Even on a bad day, you *know* the big win you and your wife have identified is worth the struggle. You *know* getting there will be tough. You *know* it won't happen overnight and that there are many more bad days standing between you and your goals. We have to train ourselves to focus more on what we know and less on what we feel. Don't follow your feelings; your feelings will fail you. Instead, decide right now, today, that you and your wife will fight through the bad days—even when you don't *feel* like it—because you know your dreams are worth the struggle.

BURN THE SHIPS

In 1519, explorer Hernán Cortés arrived in Mexico with around six hundred men. They had sailed from Cuba, where Cortés held a comfortable political position. Their goal was to explore deep into the interior of Mexico—an intimidating trek for the Spanish expedition. Upon reaching the shore, as legend has it, Cortés ordered his men to burn the ships. As they watched their only means of sea travel go up in smoke, the message was clear: quitting was not an option. No matter how difficult the Mexican exploration would be, they had no choice but to press on. Two years and a thousand struggles later, Cortés and his men succeeded in conquering the Aztec empire.

There is a huge difference between what you *know* and what you *feel*.

So, what's the point of this story? To win in network marketing, you're going to have to burn the ships. If you leave yourself an out, you'll take it. If you go into this business saying, "Let's just try it," you will quit the moment things get tough. However, if you prepare yourself for the hard days ahead, if you're strong enough to face them and bold enough to prioritize what you *know* over what you *feel*, you can achieve something significant for your family. But only if you don't quit.

SECTION 4 WRAP-UP

Before we leave this section, let's run through the high points. First, I gave you a reality check that your wife will definitely have setbacks in her business. It's not a question of *if*, but *when*. Second, we looked at a few ways we can learn from our losses and how to avoid screwing up our screwups. Third, I encouraged you to be a safe and sound husband—a safe place for her to turn to and a source of sound advice when needed. Fourth, I introduced you to your new role as hype man for her business and challenged you to bring a little Don King flair into the mix. And last, in this chapter, I tried to give you a shot in the arm to help you and your wife avoid quitting and commit to sticking it out through the hard days ahead.

Now it's time to move on to the final section of the book: Choices That Separate. There, we'll look at a few final points for building a lasting business and how to protect it for the long haul. We're in the home stretch, so stick with me!

ACTION STEP

Let's do something a little different for this action step. In honor of the "burn the ships" mentality, I want you and your wife to burn your fears—literally. Get a stack of index cards and a couple of markers. If you have a fireplace or firepit, make a fire and spend about fifteen minutes sitting in front of it as you write out every fear, excuse, obstacle, and second thought you can think of regarding her business. If there is anything that might ever encourage you to quit, write it on a card. When you're done, take turns reading one card at a time out loud. Discuss why it's a fear or potential business-killer and come up with a few ways to avoid it. Then, throw the card in the fire and watch it burn. Keep going until all your fears and excuses have gone up in smoke.

SPOTLIGHT ON SUCCESS

Frank and Patti Reed
Rodan + Fields, Level V Leaders

When my wife, Patti, approached me about getting involved in a direct sales company, my initial thought was, *Absolutely not!* I mean, everybody knows those things are scams, right? I believed what I'd always been told about network marketing: it's not a legitimate business, only the people at the very top make any real money, and all the other wrong-headed assumptions people make. I couldn't deny the results she had gotten as a customer of this particular company, though. Their products were top-quality, and the people behind the company had a stellar reputation for building a $1 billion brand. But network marketing? *Really?*

Finally, Patti asked me to simply pray about it. That caused me to pause. I realized she was serious about this and she really wanted my blessing before she got started. So, I looked into it a bit more. A week later, I was still skeptical but trusted her enough to invest some money into their midrange starter package. I honestly assumed she'd run down this rabbit trail and fizzle out. Maybe then, I figured, I could convince her to get back into her former advertising career. I thought a few hundred bucks was a small price to pay to get her to go back to work, which is what I wanted her to do.

Man, did she prove me wrong—*big time*. Her business exploded! She didn't just prove she had what it takes to be successful; she proved that network marketing can be a fantastic way to achieve our family goals. The money she's made, the perks, the flexibility, the tax advantages, the trips she's won . . . it's been a homerun! Now I can't imagine what our lives would be like *without* her network-marketing business!

SECTION 5

CHOICES THAT SEPARATE

CHAPTER 21

NO SHORTCUTS

BECKIE'S MOUTH HUNG OPEN IN SHOCK AS SHE READ THE TEXT THAT had just dinged on her phone. It was the end of the month, and she had just wrapped up her sales, team placement, and organization volume. That whole process can be like finishing a puzzle, trying to get each piece perfectly placed in just the right spot. Allocating sales and team members correctly is crucial in this business. If you don't know what you're doing, you can miss out on huge bonuses and even rank advancements. As Beckie closed out her month, she had the chance to help a builder on her team with some last-minute sales volume. That extra kick enabled this hardworking, get-it-done team member to advance in rank. She and Beckie were thrilled! Another builder on Beckie's team named Stephanie, however, was not.

When Stephanie heard that Beckie had helped another builder instead of giving that extra volume to her, she was ticked. She sent a hurtful text message accusing Beckie of all sorts of crazy things. Stephanie complained that Beckie never helped her as much as she helped other people and left her to figure things out on her own. Amazingly, she outright accused Beckie of holding her back!

When you get right down to it, do you know what made Stephanie so mad? It was that Beckie had the chance to give *someone* a boost, and she chose to give it to the builder who was already going above and beyond. For that specific month, it wasn't Stephanie. Beckie knew Stephanie could build something amazing if she would only commit to working the business the way others had done. Nothing would have made Beckie happier than to give Stephanie an extra boost every now and then, but, at that point in Stephanie's business, it wouldn't have been a *boost*; it would have been a *shortcut*. And, the truth is, an easy shortcut would have done more harm than good to Stephanie's business. She needed to boost her own efforts first, and only then would she be ready for some special assistance to take her even further.

EFFORT = RESULTS

Results in anything—especially network marketing—don't come easy. Some people get into this business looking for a fast, easy cash grab, but we've seen there is no such thing as get rich quick in network marketing. As much as I'd like to say there's a secret loophole or some kind of performance-enhancing drug your wife can take to supercharge her business, there just isn't one. You want to know the secret to building a successful business? You want to know what separates the winners from the whiners? It's *effort*. That's it. If you want to win, you've got to put in the work. There is no shortcut.

> **If you want to win, you've got to put in the work. There is no shortcut.**

It's true in business, your marriage, your health, your relationships, and every other part of your life: *effort = results*. The amount of effort you put in will determine the level of results you experience. You reap what you sow, as the saying goes. If you sow seeds of work, intentionality, and serious effort, you'll get a good crop of profit and a bigger business. If you sow seeds of laziness, excuses, and half-hearted effort, you'll grow a crop of disappointment and bitterness. That was the harvest Stephanie was sitting in. She was jealous of the bounty she saw in someone else's field, but she was never willing to do the hard work of sowing and reaping that the successful builder had done. She wanted the fruit without the farming, but that just doesn't happen.

Many people start out in network marketing expecting to make a full-time income with part-time effort, and then they blame the business model when things don't work out that way. The problem is rarely the business model. The most glaring problem I've seen in failed network-marketing businesses is the level of effort (or lack thereof) the builder is willing to put into it. If you or your wife is frustrated at the results you're getting, the best advice I can give you is to take a hard and honest look at the effort your putting into it. Bottom line: if you don't like what you've been *getting*, you've got to examine what you've been *giving*. Chances are, that's where you'll find the problem.

SACRIFICE TO WIN

Winning doesn't only require effort; it also requires sacrifice. And I'm not just talking about *your wife's* sacrifices, either. You two are a team, so you're both going to have to go into this business expecting to give some things up. It's probably a little clichéd, but this is like giving up junk food and unhealthy behaviors in order to get healthy. That's something I had to face a few years ago. I was pretty active in high school and college, but then life happened. I graduated, started my career, got married, had kids, and, suddenly, I looked down and realized I could barely see my feet over my gut. I spent about ten years in an unhealthy cycle of losing twenty-five pounds on some crazy crash diet, getting back down to my ideal weight, and then eating like a moron until I put all twenty-five pounds back on. At that point, I'd have a wake-up call, make a commitment to change, and start the lose-gain cycle all over again. I probably gained and lost the same twenty-five pounds a dozen times! This went on and on for a decade until I finally said, *Enough*.

I realized that I had spent ten years looking for a shortcut. I didn't want to eat healthy consistently, and I certainly didn't want to commit to a simple, ongoing exercise plan for the rest of my life. It wasn't until I quit the cycle and stopped looking for an easy hack that I actually made positive changes in my health. I stopped eating donuts for breakfast and a giant bowl of ice cream before bed. Trust me—those were *serious* sacrifices. I also sacrificed some free time in order to lock myself into a regular workout routine. Now, a few years later, I can honestly say I'm in the best shape I've been in since college. And no shortcut or "life hack" got me here. My health didn't change until my attitude did, until I was ready to sacrifice the short-term high for the long-term win and put in the work to make it happen.

This is exactly how it's going to be with your involvement in your wife's business. You are both going to have to make sacrifices. We've covered the practical aspect of this sacrifice in earlier chapters, but now, I really want you to embrace this

If you don't like what you've been getting, you've got to examine what you've been giving.

on an emotional level. You aren't simply sacrificing so your wife can have more time to spend "doing her thing." You're both sacrificing so you can achieve the big win you've set for your family. I'm not talking about small sacrifices, either. If you want big wins, you need to put in big effort and make big sacrifices. Author and sales legend Jim Rohn said it best: "Successful people do what unsuccessful people are unwilling to do. Don't wish it were *easier*; wish you were *better*."

As you invest in your wife's business, you will stay up too late discussing strategies and goals with her, you'll take vacation days from your normal job to invest into her business, you'll miss Saturday afternoon football games in order to spend the day brainstorming and dreaming with her, and a whole lot more. And don't expect sacrifice to get any easier. It's *always* hard to give up the things we want *now* for the things we want *most*. But that's the sacrifice it takes to win.

DO HARD THINGS

Growing a successful business doesn't just mean giving up things we *want* to do; it also means doing things we *don't want* to do. And, from what I've seen watching women operate these businesses, this is often the breaking point for many husbands. I call this choosing the *hard right* over the *easy wrong*. Some husbands, for example, are too insecure to help their wives achieve a level of success they haven't achieved for themselves, so they subtly squash their wives' potential. That's the easy wrong. You see, it's easy for some guys to excuse their own lack of motivation and effort—and therefore their lack of results—as long as their wives are

"Today I will do what others *won't* so tomorrow I can accomplish what others *can't*."

stuck in the same rut with them. However, when a strong, enterprising woman begins to outwork her husband, he may get uncomfortable. At that point, he has a choice to make: Does he get over himself, setting his inflated ego aside, and get in the trenches with his successful wife? Or, does he try to keep her down at his level so they can both wallow in their disappointment and dissatisfaction with a life that didn't turn out like they hoped?

Wallowing and whining are easy. Anybody can do that. Heaven knows we have enough examples of weak men planted on their sofas with a beer in one hand and a remote control in the other complaining about how "the little man can't get ahead." A great husband, however, does the opposite. He doesn't run from his wife's potential by mocking the business or pointing out her lack of experience. Instead, he steps up. He fuels and magnifies his wife's efforts in the hope that she achieves far greater success than he ever had so that *together* they can live the life they always dreamed about. That's the *hard right*—doing the right thing . . . even when it's hard.

DO WHAT OTHERS WON'T

Jerry Rice, the greatest wide receiver to ever play football, said, "Today I will do what others *won't* so tomorrow I can accomplish what others *can't.*" Doing what others won't comes down to three things: effort, sacrifice, and the commitment to do the right thing even when it's hard. If you've got those three things going for you, there's no limit to what you and your wife can accomplish in this business.

Your action step for this chapter is to write down one thing you will need to sacrifice in order to truly partner with your wife at the level she needs you to in her business. What will it be? A few Saturday afternoon college football games? Poker night with your buddies? A few of your precious vacation days from your regular job? What sacrifice will make the biggest impact on her business? What will mean the most to her on an emotional or relational level? Give this one some serious thought and, when you've made your decision, put that commitment in writing and share it with your wife.

CHAPTER 22

PLAY FAIR

THROUGHOUT THIS BOOK, I'VE BEEN TRYING TO HELP YOU BECOME a better teammate for your wife as she works her business. If you've noticed, becoming a better *teammate* means becoming a better *husband* in a few key areas. And, if it sounds like I'm setting myself up as a shining example of the perfect husband you should strive to become, let me cut you off right there. I want you to be *better* than I was in the early days of my wife's business. I honestly made some huge mistakes as Beckie built her business. Big ones. Giant, selfish, embarrassing screwups that any man should feel bad about.

Once I got over the initial shock that my wife joined a network-marketing company, I got on board with Beckie's plans and volunteered to help however she needed me to. I jumped in and took an active role on her team, excited that she and I had something we could do together. A few months and several new responsibilities later, though, my attitude started to tank. Even worse, I began to realize how much my reaction to her business was impacting our relationship. I thought I was doing great; in truth, I was royally screwing everything up—and something had to change.

At that point, I was leading a mastermind group with several of her business builders, taking them through a book study of different leadership books. The group met once a week on my only day off from my regular job, so it meant giving up a huge chunk of my precious free time. In addition to this, Beckie's business was experiencing a massive growth phase that demanded a lot of her time. That meant I was pulling single-parent duty at least two nights a week while she taught classes and drove all over town launching new business builders. I'd pitch in here, cover another responsibility there, and do my best to juggle all the balls we had in the air. Before long, I started keeping score—never a good sign in a marriage.

I began keeping a mental tally of all the hours I was putting in and all the responsibilities I was taking on while Beckie focused on her business. I felt a huge sense of entitlement, convincing myself of all the things I *deserved* for being such an awesome, accommodating husband. I found myself dropping hints here and there to make sure Beckie knew how much I was doing—and what I wanted in return. When there was something I wanted to buy, I never failed to remind her how much I was supporting her business efforts. When I didn't think she said *thank you* often enough, I went to bed irritated and feeling overlooked. When she came to bed a little too late or a little too tired to enjoy some "couple time," I felt unappreciated. *Doesn't she see what all I'm doing for her?* I thought. *What about me? What about what I need?* Needless to say, the voices in my head kept me from finding much peace and often made me a jerk to be around.

Around that time, a well-known NBA player made headlines for acting out on the court. He was the star player, and he wasn't shy about *acting* like the star. I'm sure you see this happen all the time, when one or two players act like they carry the entire team and think they are more important than anyone else in the organization. These guys keep track of every pass they receive and still whine about not getting the ball more often. Why? Because they fully believe they *deserve* special treatment. *What a moron,* I thought as I read the sports news. That's when it hit me: I had become the diva on Beckie's team. I was the selfish player who cared more about what he could *get* than what he could *give.*

At some point on the journey, I had stopped celebrating the fact that Beckie and I had something special we could do together, and I started seeing myself as the linchpin in her business. Even though we had set goals together and dreamed big dreams together, I had forgotten the *together* part of the deal and started focusing only on myself. I was more concerned with how the business benefited me and, more significantly, how the business interfered with my life. Rather than being a key builder, I was actually the one putting the business—and our marriage—in danger. My selfish attitude was sabotaging Beckie's hard work and stealing her momentum, and I knew she absolutely did not deserve that.

One night, as I was wrestling through all this, a sobering thought hit me right between the eyes: *What would I want or need from Beckie if the tables were turned? Who would I need her to be and how would I want her to act if I was the one building this business?* Ouch. The truth is, I'd want and need her to be the exact opposite of what I'd become. And this isn't just theory; this is actually what Beckie had been for me throughout my entire career. She'd been amazing at supporting me throughout my professional life. We'd moved several times as I advanced in my career, and she supported me every step of the way. She never griped about uprooting our family or about the nights and weekends I had to spend at church every week. She always held down the fort at home when I couldn't be there, and she even built a few successful businesses of her own along the way!

That evening, as I sat there reflecting on my bad attitude, I realized I needed to be as good a spouse as Beckie had been to me. But how?

BE THE SPOUSE YOU WANT YOUR SPOUSE TO BE

I don't want you to *survive* your wife's business; I want you, your wife, and your marriage to *thrive* as she builds it. It took a little while for me to get my head on straight after my rocky start, but I can genuinely say Beckie and I are now thriving more than ever. And, after walking so many other couples through this process, I believe the key to thriving in marriage through this business is to apply the lesson I learned the hard way: to always strive to be the spouse you want your spouse to be.

You don't want your wife to keep score, go back on her word, or complain about following through with what she told you she'd do, do you? Of course not. Well, guess what? She doesn't want you to act like that, either. If you **Be the spouse** are going to reach your full potential together **you want your** and achieve the big win you've identified, you **spouse to be.** each need to agree to do whatever it takes to become the spouse you want your spouse to be. I can think of four ways for you to do this as you work together to build her business:

1. *Pay* attention; don't *seek* attention.
2. Have an attitude of gratitude.
3. Treat her wins like your wins.
4. Go the distance.

Let's break these down a bit.

Pay Attention; Don't Seek Attention

I remember keeping count of all the different things I was doing for the business and getting irritated if Beckie only thanked me for six of the ten things I did in a week. If that's you, please—for the sake of your marriage—get over yourself. Let me be blunt: your wife *already knows* what all you're doing to support her. She gets it, just like Beckie knew everything I was doing in our first few months. Your wife may not say *thank you* for every little thing, but that doesn't mean she doesn't see how hard you're working or how much you're contributing. She doesn't need to comment on every single task you do; take her at her word when she says one meaningful, all-encompassing *thank you*.

Imagine how much more you and your wife could accomplish if you weren't so focused on getting recognized for your contributions and she wasn't so preoccupied trying to keep track of all the different things she needed to thank you for. You're *both* working hard, and you *both* get to reap the rewards of all that effort. If she overlooks one or two things you've done, just suck it up. I bet you've missed a few of the million things she's doing for your family every week, too!

Have an Attitude of Gratitude

We hear this phrase so often that I'm afraid it's lost its impact. However, if we really go through life, our marriages, and this business with an attitude of gratitude, we will always see the best in every opportunity and find new opportunities around every corner. The great Zig Ziglar said, "The more you express gratitude for what you have, the more likely you will have *even more* to express gratitude for."

Gratitude begins where entitlement ends. I wasn't feeling very grateful while I was keeping track of every task I did, sacrifice I made, and prize I thought I was entitled to. When I gave up that sense of entitlement and truly expressed gratitude for the opportunity to build something amazing with my wife, our whole business—not to mention our relationship—kicked into overdrive. So, instead of focusing on (or whining about) the sacrifices you're making, be grateful that you and your wife have the incredible opportunity to work together to build a business that can literally change your family's future!

Treat Her Wins Like Your Wins

I've mentioned this before, but it's worth repeating here. If you got a promotion at work, wouldn't you want your wife to be excited for you? If you made a big sale and earned a huge commission, wouldn't you want her to celebrate with you and tell you how proud she is of you? Of course you would! Are you doing that for her? Are you celebrating her rank advancements? Do you show your excitement when she makes a big sale or adds a new customer? If you're not, something needs to change—and *quickly*.

Remember, every step forward she takes in this business brings you both one step closer to your family's big win. That's why it is so important to work together early on to set your goals for your family. Her wins *are* your wins, because you are on this journey together.

Go the Distance

My son and I recently watched *Rocky* together. I had honestly forgotten how inspiring that movie is. In one pivotal scene, Rocky admits to his girlfriend (*Yo, Adrian!*) that he doesn't think he can beat Apollo Creed. Instead, he has a different goal. "All I want to do is go the distance," he says. "If I can go that distance, see, and that bell rings and I'm still standing, I'm gonna know for the first time in my life, see, that I weren't just another bum from the neighborhood."

Your goal is to go the distance with your wife.

In your wife's business, it's not about the pace she takes but rather that she goes the distance. That's how you win in network marketing. But it won't be a real win if you're not standing at the finish line with her. Your goal is to go the distance *with your wife*. Marriage isn't easy as it is; add in the stress of building a new business together, and you have a potential disaster on your hands. You *also* have the potential for something amazing, though, so do not quit on your wife. Go the distance with her! And when things get hard (and they will), don't hesitate to get help. Talk to a counselor or get some advice from another couple you respect. Do whatever it takes to keep fighting and going the distance together.

FOLLOW THE GOLDEN RULE

"Be the spouse you want your spouse to be" is just another way of saying, "Do to others as you would have them do to you."[13] It's the Golden Rule of marriage! Love your wife the way you want to be loved. Help your wife the way you want to be helped. Honor and celebrate your wife the way you want to be honored and celebrated. In doing so, you'll show yourself to be much more than a great business partner; you'll prove yourself to be the husband and life partner your wife deserves.

ACTION STEP

Review the four steps for becoming the spouse you want your spouse to be:

1. *Pay* attention; don't *seek* attention.
2. Have an attitude of gratitude.
3. Treat her wins like your wins.
4. Go the distance.

Put a check mark next to the one you do best and be encouraged about your good attitude in that area. Now, circle the one you need to work on the most. Write down a few practical things you can do to improve in this area. Instead of sharing this commitment with your wife as we've done with other action steps, keep this one to yourself and *show* her your commitment with your new actions and attitude.

13 Luke 6:31, NIV.

CHAPTER 23

REINVEST WISELY

JUSTINE WAS ABOUT A YEAR INTO HER BUSINESS, AND SHE'D BEEN doing great. She had worked hard, built a good customer base, and was seeing some serious momentum. By that point, Justine was consistently generating anywhere from $1,000 to $2,000 a month, which was a huge boost to their family goals of reinvesting into her business, paying off debt, saving for their kids' college, and making up some lost ground on their retirement savings. For the first time in years, Justine and her husband were able to breathe a little easier and the financial stress they'd lived with throughout their entire marriage was starting to lift.

Justine had been open with Beckie and me about their financial struggles, and we were excited for them as they seemed to be making smart decisions with her new income. Then, one day, Justine pulled into an event with a brand-new, $30,000 minivan. We were shocked! We knew they already had two good cars. Sure, they were several years old, but they worked well and had enough room for their family. Plus, they were paid off and still had plenty of life left in them. Justine and her husband, though, had gotten car fever. She explained how wonderful it felt to have a nice, new car for the first time in a long while. Beckie tried to act excited for them, but we both had so many questions. *What about their debt payoff plans? What about college and retirement savings? What about reinvesting into the business?* After having so many planning and dreaming sessions with Justine, Beckie couldn't see how a new car fit into their long-term plans.

Beckie and I talked about Justine's van later than night. We were honestly sad for her. Justine told us that the new van came with a $550 monthly payment for the next five years. That meant they'd have to dial back their other goals to make room for the new payment every month. It also meant they wouldn't have much (if any) money to reinvest into growing her business. Justine and her husband had gotten a taste of the extra income that network marketing could provide, and they blew it. Just as things started to get better for them, they put themselves right back into financial stress with a giant new monthly payment and five-year commitment hanging over their heads. In a sense, they were just as bad off as they were before. The financial pressure and money fights were probably going to be worse than ever, and our friend wasn't going to have the margin she needed to take her business to the next level. From our perspective, this van situation was a total loss.

What Justine did was incredibly common in America today. In fact, you could even consider it *normal* behavior. Like financial expert Dave Ramsey often says, "Most people tend to celebrate a $400 pay raise by getting a new $500 car payment!" Can you see the problem with that? Making bad decisions with new income can actually make your financial situation *worse*. It gives us new opportunities to do some really dumb things. That's why, in this chapter, I want to present a countercultural message about what to do with your wife's new network-marketing income. I want these new resources to leave you better off than you were before, so let's spend a few minutes talking about the magic of reinvestment.

THE REINVESTMENT CYCLE

As you and your wife build her business, especially if you follow the advice in this book, you're going to have some extra income coming in. So ... what are you going to do with it? You should have already identified your key goals and big win for your family, so how can you stay focused on those things once the money starts rolling in?

The overriding principle for your new salary is simple: use your income to create more *margin*, not more *pressure*. Use it to create more freedom, not more restrictions. The typical American family already has an endless list of restrictions. We have no extra time, money, or freedom to do anything! We don't get enough rest, we always seem to be strapped for cash, we're overworked and over-stressed, and we spend countless hours doing things we hate. And, when we do get a new influx of money, it all seems to slip through our fingers. We use it to buy things we don't need or take big, expensive vacations we can't really afford.

Use your income to create more *margin*, not more *pressure*.

Then, when the cash is gone, we find ourselves right back where we started. No matter how much money we make, nothing ever seems to improve! You and your wife should make it your goal to change all that with her new income—but that will only happen when you handle this money with a plan.

I want to suggest a simple plan for taking control of the money you and your wife generate through her business. I call it the Reinvestment Cycle, and it's easy to understand but deceptively hard to stick to. The point of the cycle is to break the bad habits most of us have when we get our hands on a pay raise. You see, most people work to make money, but then they waste that money on stuff that doesn't add real value to their lives. This causes them to have the same level of stress (if not more) and the same lack of free time. This sends them back to work with depleted levels of time and energy. Then they make more money, waste it on more crap, deal with more stress, and go back to work even more bogged down. Rinse and repeat. Sound familiar? No wonder most people can't stand the sound of the alarm clock on Monday mornings. They're trapped in an endless loop they can't escape from, like a hamster stuck running on his little wheel.

The only way to change what you've been *getting* is to change what you've been *doing*.

The only way to change what you've been *getting* is to change what you've been *doing*. You need a new plan, so try this. Instead of wasting the new income that's coming in, use it to recapture more time and energy. That's what the four steps of the Reinvestment Cycle do for you. It's an ongoing cycle in which you:

1. *Make money*, which you can then . . .
2. *Reinvest wisely* on things that enable you to . . .
3. *Recapture more time and energy*, which you can then . . .
4. *Reinvest into your business.*

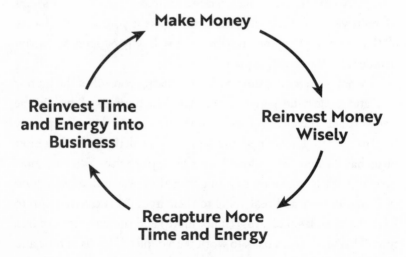

It's not rocket science, but it can breathe new life into your family and eliminate much of the financial stress you may have thought was permanent.

The key to sustained success and financial relief isn't more money. If you aren't prepared to handle it wisely, more money can (and probably will) do more harm than good. No, the real secret sauce of changing your family's financial situation is the powerful combo of time and energy. If you use your income to recapture more time and energy, life will instantly get better for you. Stress will go down and satisfaction will go up. When you reinvest some of that time and energy into the business, you'll make even *more* money, which enables you to create even more time and energy. This takes some effort early in the business, but a commitment to start things well will generate momentum that will drive your business for years to come and give you a greater life than you ever imagined!

THREE PRINCIPLES FOR REINVESTMENT

This may sound like a lot of hype so far, so I'll spend the rest of this chapter discussing a few practical ways to get the Reinvestment Cycle spinning in your wife's business. If you want to reinvest this money wisely and use it to generate new levels of time and energy for your family, you need to adopt three foundational principles. Let's break them down.

Live Below Your Means
Most people are up to their eyeballs in debt. The average American, in fact, has about $38,000 in personal debt, not counting their home mortgage.[14] That's a mix of credit cards,

14 Megan Leonhardt, "Here's how much debt Americans have at every age," CNBC, August 20, 2018, https://www.cnbc.com/2018/08/20/how-much-debt-americans-have-at-every-age.html.

student loans, car loans, personal loans, and other consumer credit items. Unbelievably, CNBC found that two in ten Americans spend 50 to 100 percent of their monthly income on debt payments![15] How on earth can any of us get ahead financially if we keep spending all our money on debt payments? Is that really the American Dream so many of us are chasing?

This is not a book on personal finance, and I don't want to get too preachy about debt. However, I can say with confidence that bad money management can destroy your wife's business.

If you use your income to recapture more time and energy, life will instantly get better for you.

In fact, poor money management is the number one reason why most small businesses fail within the first five years.[16] If you spend every dime she makes, you'll have nothing left to use to grow the business and give it a solid foundation for the future. But at least you'll have some fun for a few years before she's forced to close the business, right? Wrong. Believe it or not, your wife's new income could actually bring more financial stress into your family if you aren't prepared to handle it well. It would be such a waste if the only thing your family had to show for all your wife's hard work was a new car payment and even greater levels of financial stress.

Debt is a huge problem in this country, and I personally believe you'll never win financially until you get rid of your debt once and for all and make the sacrifices required to create financial margin in your life. If you need help (and most people do), I encourage you to

15 Ibid.
16 Michael Flint, "Cash Flow: The Reason 82% of Small Businesses Fail," Preferred CFO, March 8, 2018, https://www.preferredcfo.com/cash-flow-reason-small-businesses-fail/.

check out *The Total Money Makeover* by Dave Ramsey.[17] He also has an excellent live and online class called *Financial Peace University* that has helped millions of people—including Beckie and me—turn their financial lives around.

Recapture Time and Energy

What tasks do you and your wife do that you absolutely hate? What chores suck the life out of you and ruin your day? Think about things like cleaning the house, cutting the grass, doing laundry, shopping for groceries, and grooming your dog. It shouldn't take you long to figure out what you hate doing!

Now, let me ask you this: how much time and energy would you recapture if you actually paid someone else to do those things? For some people, the thought of paying someone else to clean their house sounds crazy, but this can be one of the best investments your wife could make in her business. Remember, time and energy are the keys to building a long-term, rewarding busi-

Use your *money* to buy *margin*.

ness. If cleaning the house or doing laundry eats up her precious time and leaves her feeling drained and irritated, why on earth would you not want her to reclaim that lost time and energy? If she used some of her business income to hire a housekeeper for a few hours a week, she could then use that time to work on her business. This is what it means to use your *money* to buy *margin*. Giving yourself permission and managing your money wisely enough to do this is truly life-changing!

That extra time—not to mention the energy and joy she'd get from spending her time doing something she actually *enjoys*—would create exponential results in her business. Translation: she'd make more money *and* avoid miserable work that steals her time and

17 Dave Ramsey, *The Total Money Makeover* (Nashville: Thomas Nelson, 2007).

energy. It's a win-win! That's when the Reinvestment Cycle really gets humming! Besides, if you try this and it doesn't work out or feels like too much of a financial strain, you can just stop. Paying a housekeeper to come for a trial run one afternoon is a much safer bet than signing up for sixty months of car payments you can't get out of!

Reward Your Team

Finally, wise management of your business income should always include some reinvestment back into your team members in the form of rewards. When you have financial margin, your wife can send her team members books and resources every now and then to help them grow their businesses. She can send them small gifts to recognize rank advancements or even cash surprises when they hit their goals. These gestures are incredibly motivating to team members and can breathe new life into their businesses. And of course, one of the joys of network marketing is that *you* benefit when *they* benefit. Imagine your wife giving a team member a $20 sales and networking book that resulted in $50 more income *every month*. That's a pretty good investment, and I see that type of thing happen every day in my wife's business. Beyond the potential for more income, this is a great way to remind team members that you and your wife value them and support them in everything they're doing to build strong businesses of their own.

ENJOY SOME REWARDS

I hope this chapter challenged some of your preconceptions about your wife's new business income, and I *really* hope it stopped you from wasting your money. However, I don't want you to think there's no room for you or your wife to enjoy her success. As important as it is for her to reinvest money back into her business and into her team members, it's just as important to make small, meaningful reinvestments back into herself and your family. One big way you can do this is by reclaiming time and energy, which we discussed in this chapter. Another way is through a few extravagances every now and then. This could be a spa day, a weekend trip with her girlfriends, or—better yet—a romantic getaway for the two of you. I don't suggest making this a big part of your financial life, but some surprises every now and then won't hurt. In fact, you'll be amazed at how much these small indulgences will energize her, communicate how much you care about her, and encourage her to take her business to even greater heights!

ACTION STEP

Ask your wife to read this chapter and discuss the following questions together:

1. What is stealing our financial margin and creating unwanted stress in our lives?
2. Do we need to do something radical to free up some time, energy, and money?
3. What tasks or chores do we absolutely hate doing?
4. How much would it cost to pay someone to do one or two of these things? How can we make that fit into our business plan?
5. What are some small ways we can reward or incentivize our team members as they grow their businesses?

CHAPTER 24

PRIORITIZE HER GROWTH

BECKIE WAS A WHIRLWIND OF ACTIVITY IN THE FIRST FEW MONTHS of her business. Of course, she was meeting with people, going to classes, setting up her organization, selling product, and doing all kinds of administrative work—I expected that from the start. I know she's the kind of woman who goes all-in once she makes a commitment, so I wasn't surprised at how hard she worked to get things moving. What did surprise me, though, was how much time she spent on personal development activities. She was unrelenting in her commitment to dedicate one or two hours every day to her personal growth. Practically every day when I got home from work, she was finishing a new book or wrapping up some online teaching or podcast series. At that time, I thought it was overkill. Looking back, though, I can see that Beckie knew how important her own growth would be to the overall growth of her business. If she hadn't prioritized personal development over other things—things that probably felt more *urgent* in the moment—she never would have been able to sustain her rapid growth.

If you ask any woman who's trying to build a network-marketing business if she thinks personal growth is important, she'll almost certainly say yes. But if you ask her what she's doing for personal growth and how often she sets time aside for it, the discussion will change. She'll probably get a sheepish look on her face and say something like, "Well, I know I *should* be reading or listening to something every day, but life is just so busy. I'm lucky to get my orders logged and my kids' teeth brushed before I collapse into bed at night!" Sadly, everyone thinks it's a good idea, but almost no one is doing it. It reminds me of an old Chinese proverb, "Talk doesn't cook rice." You can talk about it all you want, but how you spend your time shows what you really value.

How you spend your time shows what you really value.

The hard truth is, there's only one reason why you and your wife don't spend any time during the week improving yourselves: personal development is not important enough to you for you to prioritize it over other things. It's time to change that.

THREE PRIORITIES FOR GROWTH

As I've led teams of people throughout my career and especially now that I've watched Beckie lead a large network-marketing business, I've come to believe every professional should hold onto three specific priorities no matter how busy life gets. Each of these priorities will demand some time and, occasionally, some money. However, it's an investment that pays huge dividends. The best investment, they say, is an investment in yourself. So, what are the three priorities that will make your wife a better network marketer and make you a better network-marketing husband? It all comes down to resources, experiences, and people. Let's break them down a bit.

Prioritize Resources
You've probably heard the phrase "Leaders are readers" or "Leaders are learners." I've probably heard it fifty times throughout my career. Cliché or not, it's 100 percent true. The women I know who lead

some of the largest network-marketing teams in the country are the most voracious readers I've ever seen. They devour every book, article, training video, online workshop, podcast, and class they can get their hands on. The Information Age has put a world of information at our fingertips. Practically *anyone* can become an expert on *anything* at *any time*—right from the comfort of their own living room. With so many resources available to us today, there is no excuse for not investing in personal growth.

And if you and your wife say you don't have enough time, try this little hack: Commit to investing twenty minutes to some personal development resource every day *before* you allow yourself to watch TV or check social media. You'd be shocked at what you can accomplish in only twenty minutes. It adds up too. If you did this every day, you'd add one hundred and twenty-one hours of personal development time to your "busy" schedule every year! So, put it on the calendar—and stick to it. And, as a great husband, it's your job to honor and protect the time your wife has set aside to improve herself. Who wouldn't want a more confident, intelligent, and successful wife? All it takes is a little time devoted to the right resources.

Prioritize Experiences

As good as books, videos, audio, and other resources are, they still can't get you quite as pumped and make as strong an emotional impact as real, in-person, face-to-face interactions with like-minded people. That's where your company's live training events come in. All the quality network-marketing companies I know offer amazing training experiences for their business builders, and they often encourage spouses to come, as well. At the very least, your wife *has* to attend her company's annual convention every year. Nothing will energize her and boost her belief in her organization more than joining thousands of other builders from across the country in their biggest, most exciting, most inspirational blowout event of the year.

Some of the larger network-marketing companies also add regional training opportunities throughout the year. These are a great time to get together with other builders and their spouses as you learn the ins and outs of the business and, more importantly, build community with other men and women going through the exact same challenges and opportunities that your family is going through. Keep in mind that annual conventions and regional training will cost a little money—usually a convention fee plus travel, meals, and lodging. However, these things are *not* a waste of money; you should think of them as necessary business expenses and encourage your wife to attend as many as she can (without breaking the bank, of course).

As your wife levels up, she will probably gain access to exclusive training experiences designed to help her build on the momentum she's generated. These are often beautiful, all-expenses-paid trips and can be incredible weekend getaways for you as a couple. Remember, I was on one of these trips when I got the inspiration to write this book. It's hard to be around that many hard-charging, successful entrepreneurs and not come away motivated to put a little extra into your work. These experiences are rarer and usually must be earned, so don't let her miss out when she scores an invitation to one.

And listen, I hate to even have to say this, but I've seen these conversations go sideways too many times not to at least throw out a word of caution. When you wife wants to go to one of these key business events, don't make her feel bad about leaving town for a few days to focus on her personal and business development. Too many men steal all the joy and excitement from their wives' experiences by making fun of the event or making them feel guilty for leaving. Don't. Just . . . don't. We're better than that, right? So, let's skip the guilt trips and encourage our wives to make the most of every experience they can take in.

Prioritize People

We know that resources and experiences are both fundamentally important to your wife's personal and professional growth. But you know what makes an even *greater* impact? People. Specifically, the people you and your wife choose to spend time with. In my experience as a pastor and a network-marketing husband, I've found that the people you surround yourself with are both a mirror and a map. They're a mirror that shows you *who you are* and a map that shows you *where you're going*. If you ever wonder how other people see you and what potential you have in life, just look at your friends Chances are, you're just like them.

If you and your wife constantly surround yourself with world-class, successful people, you've got it made. Sadly, though, most of us have some people around us who wouldn't make that cut. So, even though this can be tricky (if not downright painful), it's time to take a close look at the people we've prioritized in our lives. But let's keep it positive. I want you to think about the three to five best friends and greatest personal influences in your lives. Think about how they navigate their marriages, careers, and finances. What are they doing that's truly extraordinary? How do they encourage you and your wife to be better people? Is this how other people would describe you? These people are your *mirror*; they show you who you are.

The people you surround yourself with are both a mirror and a map.

Now, think about a few couples or individuals that you and your wife truly respect. These can be people who are a little older than you or who are simply a little further along in their marriages or personal growth. How are you leveraging the lessons these mentors are teaching you? What can you do to make sure your life stays on a similar path as theirs, ensuring you end up where they are now? These men and women are your *map*; they show you where you're going.

It's fun thinking about and appreciating the wonderful, positive people in our lives. However, not everyone we know lives up to this standard, do they? It seems like everyone has *that guy* who's a drain on every relationship. You know, the person who complains about everything, who dismisses every opportunity, who writes off your wife's business as a scam, who says no one *really* makes money in this business, and who genuinely seems to hate his own life (and wants you to hate yours too). I don't even need to ask you to think about this person; I'm pretty sure you're already thinking about him or her.

Prioritizing people doesn't mean cutting some people *out* and trying to hook new, successful, "pretty" people *into* our lives. It does mean being intentional about who we allow into our spheres of influence. If there's a successful couple you and your wife would like to spend more time with, then make it happen. Identify who they are and try to get to know them a little better. These may already be acquaintances that you simply want to *promote* into good friends. That's a great goal—but there's a flip side. What about the less-than-positive people in our lives? That's where things get a little tricky. Your wife doesn't necessarily have to eliminate that negative friend who steals her joy . . . but she could *demote* her. Demoting a friend simply means limiting the amount of time—and therefore influence—we give someone. Chances are, you have a few friends in your life who should probably be demoted.

You only have so much time to spend with friends and influencers; make sure you're investing that time wisely by prioritizing the beneficial relationships and deprioritizing the bad ones. No, you don't have to completely cut off the buddy who acts the same at forty-two as he did at twenty-two, but he might not deserve as much of your time now as he did then. You could cut him back to a few conversations a year and trade out that time with someone who's prepared to speak success into your life.

GROWING LEADERS

I've spent an entire chapter on prioritizing your and your wife's personal growth, but I need to let you in on a little secret. Your wife's personal growth isn't so *personal*. Your wife is a network marketer, and, at the end of the day, every network marketer is a leader. It's the nature of the business; if she's winning at network marketing, it's because she's recruited a team of like-minded, go-getter women to join her on her crusade. That makes her a leader.

What difference does this make to personal growth? Simple: Everything your wife does—every book she reads, every class she takes, every training she goes to, every convention she attends—doesn't just impact her. It also impacts her team. All those lessons and learnings flow *through* her and down to them. So, when she spends an hour reading a leadership book, she's making an investment not only in herself but also in every woman on her team. She's improving her entire network. That results in a well-trained, well-led team of professionals who are each participating in your wife's success. I can't think of any other business model that provides such a direct and widespread impact!

Your wife's personal growth isn't so personal.

Personal growth matters. It's how we become better people, better spouses, better business builders, and better leaders. So, work with your wife to prioritize the resources, experiences, and people in your lives, making sure you both make the most of every opportunity to grow into the powerhouse couple and business builders you want to be!

ACTION STEP

Together with your wife, create a short list of:

1. *Resources* to begin reading/watching/listening to together. Also note how many hours you will spend on them each week.
2. *Experiences* she (and maybe you) need to participate in. Attach dates and dollar amounts to these so you can plan accordingly.
3. *People* to promote or demote in your life. Schedule time to hang out with the people you've chosen to promote.

CHAPTER 25

#1 FAN

THROUGHOUT THIS BOOK, I'VE TOLD YOU SEVERAL STORIES ABOUT how husbands totally blew it when it came to supporting their wives' network-marketing businesses. In fact, I've even told you a few stories about how I personally screwed up throughout Beckie's journey. That's called being human; we're all going to mess things up occasionally. The good news is that your wife already knows you aren't perfect. Beckie sure knows *her* husband isn't. However, every now and then, I manage to get something just right. As I've learned to keep my eyes open to what Beckie's working on and going through, I've been able to create a few very special memories for her—celebrations that stand out for her and have marked milestone moments throughout her network-marketing career. Let me tell you about one time when—fortunately—I absolutely *nailed it*.

It was the infamous last day of the month. You should know what that means by this point. It had been a crazy month, and Beckie had worked her tail off. She was exhausted—*we all were*—but she hit all her sales and building goals. The whole family pitched in that month to help her crush her goals, and we were honestly glad the month was over. Beckie had to teach a class that evening, so she spent the day closing out her month. When the dust settled, she realized that what she planned and hoped for had actually happened: she was going to end the month at Diamond level. Every network-marketing company has different names for different levels, so let me put this in perspective. At this level, Beckie had positioned herself to consistently earn $10,000 per month! This was a *huge* deal for all of us. Beckie had sacrificed, I had sacrificed . . . heck, even our kids had sacrificed to help their mother hit this mark. And now we knew all that hard work and sacrifice had paid off. Beckie was a Diamond!

When Beckie left that evening to teach her class, the kids and I created a plan to show Beckie how proud we were of her. We decided to turn every square inch of our kitchen into diamond extravaganza! We jumped in the car and drove to the local party supply store and demolished their wedding aisle. We scooped up every single diamond-themed decoration in the store and raced back home to decorate. The kids completely covered the kitchen table with diamond crafts. We scattered little plastic diamonds over every surface. Diamond ring helium balloons floated through the air and sparkly streamers hung from the ceiling and kitchen entryway. We capped it off with some homemade banners that read, "CONGRATULATIONS!," "YAY MOM," and "YOU DID IT!" With the kitchen sparkling in fake diamonds and genuine excitement, we sat down and anxiously waited for her to come home.

If you truly want to support your network-marketing wife, you've got to make sure she knows you're her number one fan.

My children were *pumped*. Truth be told, so was I. I was so proud of Beckie, and she deserved to be celebrated. I felt like I had organized the most important pep rally in history, and it was all for her. After what felt like forever, we finally heard the garage door open and raced to the kitchen to surprise her. Beckie opened the door, took a step inside, and then stopped dead in her tracks when she saw the diamond palace we had created for her. The most beautiful smile I have ever seen slowly spread across her face and—wait for it—she started to cry! *Yes! Husband for the win!*

If she didn't know before, Beckie realized in that moment that I was her number one fan. No one can cheer louder, longer, or more passionately for her than I can. Even though I had blown other key moments in her journey, I'm grateful to have gotten this one right.

We've covered a lot of ground throughout this book. We've gone through twenty-four different chapters, topics, and action steps so far, and they're all important. However, if you do all those things but miss this final step, you'll have missed the whole point. If you truly want to support your network-marketing wife, you've got to make sure she knows you're her number one fan.

THREE FAN BEHAVIORS

By now, you have learned pretty much everything you need to know to support your wife. You trust that the business model is legitimate, you've worked together to set goals and a good pace, you learned how the comp plan works, you've committed to be both her *corner man* and her *hype man*, you understand the seasons and rhythms of the business, and so much more. If you've been keeping up with me so far—reading the five sections of this book over the last five weeks—you should be *killing it* by now. All of that is crucial to her success, but the crowning jewel of all your support will be your level of fandom. You've got to be the biggest, loudest, most embarrassingly excited fan your wife has ever seen. I'm talking giant foam fingers and full-body paint levels of enthusiasm for who she is and what she's doing!

You know your wife better than anyone, so I can't tell you *exactly* what type of fan behaviors would work best for you two. However, I can give you three general behaviors that work for pretty much everyone. If you don't know where to start in showing your enthusiasm for your wife, try these.

Celebrate Her Victories

This is the most basic level of fandom—celebrating your wife's victories. That means making a big deal of her wins as she works to grow her business. The celebration doesn't have to be expensive, but it should be both *intentional* and *significant*. Don't just throw something together at the last minute; think through when and how you'll surprise her at the different stages of her business. If you're communicating well every week, you should know when she's approaching key milestones. They should rarely catch you by surprise if you and your wife are planning well and working together. So, if you know a big moment is on the horizon, get ready for it! Your wife is working her tail off trying to get there; the least you can do is be ready at the finish line with a megaphone to cheer her on.

And if you have kids, include them in the celebration. Make this a family affair! Remember, your wife isn't just working for herself and her personal goals; she's working to help the family, to bring all of you closer to your goals. Besides, it's so empowering for children to see their parents work hard for something and then achieve it. That's how kids learn how to work and how to commit to long-term goals. They need to see that hard work pays off, and they need to feel a sense of celebration when a hardworking parent hits her goals. Plus, many network-marketing moms feel guilty about the time they spend on the business instead of with their children. They need to know their kids are with them on the journey and celebrating their victories. You may be her *biggest* fan, but that doesn't mean she doesn't need to see *little* fans running around the house, too.

Say It When You See It

I always feel a little uncomfortable when I see a screaming lunatic fan on the sidelines of a sporting event before a game. As my friends and I walk through the stadium and find our seats, I can see that

99.99 percent of the people are just like me: normal men and women who just came to see a good game and show some support for the home team. But then there's that other .01 percent: the total nut jobs decked out in weird costumes—or worse, running around shirtless and covered in body paint—who are already screaming their heads off as close to the field as possible an hour before the game even starts. Those guys fascinate me. What kind of wild, uncontrollable enthusiasm must they feel for their team? What could make a mild-mannered businessman lose his mind like that for four hours every Sunday afternoon?

As much as these crazed fans freak me out, I know I have a lot to learn from them. They go *all out*. They hold nothing back when they see their team hit the field. When they see their favorite player make a big play, they erupt in applause. When they see a rookie complete a career-making catch, they go nuts. They don't care who's watching and they show no outward signs of embarrassment or inhibition. They are there first and foremost to be a fan, pure and simple. I would love to show that kind of fan dedication to my wife. I'd love for her to see me cheering her on every time she takes the field in her business. Why are we so generous with our praise to strangers throwing a football but so stingy when it comes to celebrating our own wives as they try to enrich our families' lives? That's not the way a number one fan behaves. Instead, be quick with an encouraging word and a high five every time your wife makes a play. Make sure she knows you're watching her win.

Make sure she knows you're watching her win.

Speak Her Language

Being the best *for* her means *bringing out* the best *in* her. As her number one fan, you want your wife to perform at the top of her game all the time. She can only do that if you've helped create a safe home base where she feels loved, appreciated, and understood. This is no small feat and it's far outside the scope of this book, but I can at least point you in the right direction. No resource has been as helpful to Beckie and me in improving our communication, love, and appreciation than Gary Chapman's incredible book *The Five Love Languages*.[18] He teaches that people are naturally prone to express love in one of five ways: acts of service, touch, words of affirmation, gifts, or quality time. If you and your wife seem to send and receive mixed signals (or the wrong signals) all the time, it's

> **Being the best *for* her means *bringing* *out* the best *in* her.**

probably because you aren't speaking the right language. Chapman's book can help cut through the static and teach you how to connect with each other like never before. That might be the perfect follow-up book for you after you finish this one.

BUT TIM...

When I cover the "number one fan" point with some husbands, I often get pushback. "But Tim," they say, "my wife doesn't act like *my* biggest fan. How can I act like hers?" Or maybe, "But Tim, she's been pretty selfish about this whole business thing." And, of course, "But Tim, she hasn't involved me in the business at all. Why should I poke my nose into it and cheer her on now?" I get it. I know every marriage is in a different place. Some couples are deliriously happy and the business makes it better; some couples are at each other's throats and the business is just the latest weapon in the arsenal. There's no one-size-fits-all piece of advice here.

All I can say is that it is our duty as husbands to strive to support our wives in whatever they do. If it's something she's

---

18 Gary Chapman, *The Five Love Languages* (Chicago: Northfield Publishing, 1995).

deemed important, it should be important to you. Besides, I never said you had to become *network marketing's* number one fan; this is about being your *network marketing wife's* number one fan.

Take it from a guy who's already made plenty of mistakes at this: cheering your wife on in her business will change your marriage for the better. She doesn't need or want you to be her critic; she needs you to be her biggest fan—the guy who never stops cheering for her and pushing her on to bigger and better victories ahead!

SECTION 5 WRAP-UP

You just completed the last section of the book. Great job! Before we wrap everything up, let's look back over the key lessons from this section. First, we saw that there are no shortcuts in this business and that your wife's results will be tied directly to her efforts. Second, I stressed the importance of playing fair by being the kind of spouse you want your spouse to be. Third, we discussed how to reinvest wisely to grow the business and create more margin (time and energy) for your wife. Fourth, I encouraged you to prioritize her growth by maximizing key resources, experiences, and people. And finally, in this chapter, we got a glimpse of what it means to be your wife's biggest fan. If you try to support her without that last piece, you'll leave a giant hole right in the middle of your marriage!

She doesn't need or want you to be her critic; she needs you to be her biggest fan.

All that's left now is to complete this chapter's action step and review a few remaining tips. We'll do that in the final chapter next.

ACTION STEP

As you wrap up this book, I want you to do something extra special to show your wife that you are her number one fan. Here are a few ideas to get you started:

1. Order a customized giant foam finger with her name on it and bring it out on milestone moments.
2. Make or order a personalized t-shirt or hat that says, "[*wife's name*]'s #1 Fan!"
3. Write her a meaningful, handwritten note telling her how proud you are, how much you believe in her, and how honored you are to be her number one fan.

Take this further by finding new ways to do this over and over in the years ahead. This doesn't even have to center around her business; you can and should make sure she knows how much you celebrate her for everything she is and everything she does for the rest of your lives!

John and Michelle Bishop
AdvoCare Double Diamond Distributors

My wife, Michelle, and I were first introduced to our network-marketing opportunity when we were dating. I was working six to seven days a week in my regular job, so I didn't have much time to put into the new business. Michelle, however, jumped all-in. I supported her in the beginning, thinking it was just a fun side job but never imagining she'd make any real money doing it. But then, she started building *fast*. Her network-marketing income kept going up and up, inching closer to what I was making in my "real" job. That's when I screwed up. I felt threatened by how well she was doing and started taking jabs at the network-marketing industry. I made all the common jokes about multi-level marketing, telling her that her success couldn't last. It wasn't until she flew off to Italy on a trip she earned with other top leaders that I finally woke up to the reality of network marketing. I had to face the facts: it's the real deal, and Michelle was a superstar.

A few months later, on a flight to our wedding destination, I apologized for how I'd been acting and told her I wanted to work with her as a team on her business. I admitted that my bruised ego was the only reason I had criticized her business. She burst into tears of joy! All she ever wanted was for us to do this thing together.

Once we were on the same page, nothing could stop us. We earned several awards for hitting key ranks in our business, some of which we earned faster than anyone ever had. Today, we've been in the business for six years, and it's become our full-time business. More than that, my eyes are open to how incredible my wife really is. She can do *anything* with that beautiful, creative mind of hers, and I'll stand behind any one of her ideas with full confidence, faith, and encouragement.

There's no doubt about it: I am my wife's biggest fan!

AFTERWORD

IF YOU'RE READING THIS PAGE, I KNOW YOUR WIFE HAS THE TEAM-
mate she needs to excel in network marketing. I told you at the
beginning that I assume your wife bought this book or got it from
one of her upline leaders and then promptly dropped it in your lap
when she got home. So, the fact that you're *here*—reading the final
chapter of the book—tells me everything I need to know about you.
You're *awesome*. You're a good man, and I really appreciate you
sticking with me through this journey. More importantly, so does
your wife.

She's busting her butt trying to build something that will
improve your lives. She's caught a vision for a product or service she
believes can help a whole bunch of people. Maybe it's already helped
you and your family. I haven't told you this yet, but that's actually
how Beckie got involved in her company. When our daughter was
four years old, she developed a strange growth on her face. Doctors
were stumped and decided to remove it, but it grew right back less
than a month after the surgery. It was embarrassing for our daughter
even at such a young age. The day she came home from preschool
crying because someone made fun of it broke our hearts.

Around that time, a teacher noticed the problem and tentatively
suggested a product she used as a possible solution. It sounded a little
weird to us at the time, but we were willing to try anything. She gave
us a small sample and told us to use one drop three times a day. We
could see visible results within twenty-four hours. Within a week,

the growth had shrunk up to just a scab, turned black, and fell off my daughter's face. And then . . . it never came back.

Beckie and I were blown away that an obscure product a friend told us about could have such an immediate and profound impact on our child's health. That experience sent Beckie into a research frenzy that further solidified her belief in this product. She also grew to love the network-marketing company that produced and sold the health products that had begun changing our lives.

You see, despite all the naysayers and critics, network marketing isn't about trapping your friends into awkward conversations or chasing down strangers in the mall to tell them about your "opportunity." Network marketing is about building a business around a product or service you believe in. After seeing our daughter's incredible results, it was easy for Beckie to champion her product and, as a result, build a huge business around it.

That's our story. Maybe your wife had a similar experience. Maybe she was so blown away by a product that she simply *had* to tell other people about it. If you're going to go on and on to your friends about how incredible something is, you might as well make a little money doing it, right? That way, you aren't just improving other people's lives by recommending a great product; you're also improving your own family's lives by increasing your income and working toward you big-win goals. That's what I really love about this business: when done correctly (the way we've discussed in this book), network marketing is a win–win all the way around.

A FINAL WARNING

I don't need to champion network marketing to you anymore than I already have. I'm sure you can tell by now that I'm a big fan. I've seen far too many women build incredible businesses to be a skeptic any longer. However, before we wrap things up, there is one final warning I want to give you as a supportive network-marketing husband. Keep your eyes on your wife's business—and *only* your wife's business. As you and your wife grow in this business, you'll no doubt get to know other couples who are working toward their own goals through network marketing. Some of these women will seem much further along than your wife, and others will seem much further behind. So what?

We, as men, sometimes measure a person's worth by what they've accomplished professionally. Even worse, we sometimes measure *our own worth* by what we've accomplished compared to someone else. When it comes to watching our wives grow in their businesses, we can therefore be a little prone to judging her success against the success other women have had in the business. I've seen many, many husbands blow it on this point. They may say things like, "I heard Linda already made Gold rank. I guess she got things moving a lot faster than you did." Or maybe, "Why is Beth already so much further along than you are? Didn't you start at the same time?" We might even try to be encouraging by saying something like, "Honey, you're doing great! You're already making twice as much at your sister—and she's the one who brought you into the business!" I can't say it any plainer than this: *Do not do this!*

Comparison doesn't help anyone with anything. In fact, comparing her business to someone else's will likely only result in either pride or depression. If she's chosen a faster pace than another woman, she can feel prideful about outpacing that person—even though that other woman may have intentionally chosen a slower pace. Or, if your wife has chosen to go slow herself, she can feel bad about how much further along others have gotten in the same amount of time. She might be tempted to adjust her throttle based not on what works for her but on some embarrassment-driven desire to keep up with someone else. Either way, comparison is not the goal.

When you cut the comparisons and make the right decisions for *your* family—not someone else's—you will set a pace that keeps your wife motivated, engaged, and moving forward one step at a time, no matter how quickly (or slowly) she takes those steps. If you ever feel yourself losing sight of this, go back to Chapter 4 and review what we said about picking the right pace for your business. Remember, your wife chose the pace that works best for her; other women will choose different paces for different reasons. As long as each woman is hitting the personalized goals she's set for herself, they can all be winning—even if some seem to be moving faster or slower than others.

BUILD AROUND THE HOME TEAM

As your wife continues to build, she's going to add more and more people to her team. Before long, she could have dozens of women working alongside her, each one contributing to your family's big win. That's an amazing feeling, to be part of a huge network of people who are all pushing each other forward. As incredible as that team dynamic is, though, it will only be as strong as your home-team roots. You and your wife are *the* team. I don't care how many people she brings on board, and I don't care how involved her upline leaders are in her business. *You* will always be her most important business partner and teammate. No matter how hands-on (or hands-off) you are, no one will have a bigger impact on her business than you.

The good news is that, if you've read this book and done all the action steps, you have everything you need to support your wife in the way she needs you to. And you can always grab it off the shelf again whenever a new struggle or question comes up. If you find her struggling to move up in rank, go back to Chapter 14 and review what it takes to level up. When the summer slump is discouraging you both, review what Chapter 11 says about the different seasons of the business. When you aren't sure if you're helping enough, check out your sweet spot contributions in Chapter 8. When she experiences a sharp increase in income, be sure to review what Chapter 23 says about reinvesting wisely back into the business. This book was designed to give you the big picture of network marketing, and each chapter is a piece of that puzzle. When something gets off track or just plain weird in the business, come back to this book to find the answer. Then get back in the game with your wife, building a business that takes you both closer to your family goals, closer to your big win, and, most importantly, closer *together*.

Remember, this business isn't *her thing*. It's *your thing* too. This is your chance to show your wife how much you love and support her, so make it count!

ABOUT THE AUTHOR

 TIM FARRANT KNOWS WHAT IT TAKES TO SUPPORT A hard-charging, get-it-done network-marketing pro; he had a front-row seat to his wife's meteoric rise in one of the nation's premier network-marketing organizations. But Tim's no slouch, either. With more than twenty years in pastoral ministry and church leadership, Tim has led huge initiatives and personally counseled hundreds of married couples. Through personal experience and countless hours coaching other couples, Tim knows what makes a marriage work—and what tears it apart.

When he's not at work or working with his wife, Beckie, on her business, Tim is either traveling or watching football. He's visited forty-nine of the fifty states (sorry, North Dakota), and he's been to twenty-six of the thirty-one NFL stadiums. As a lifelong, diehard University of Michigan fan, Tim navigates life in enemy territory in Columbus, Ohio.

Find out more about Tim and Beckie's journey at www.networkmarketinghusband.com.